Trans Life SURVIVORS

Walt Heyer

Table of Contents

Introduction

Trans Life Survivors showcases emails from thirty or so people, selected from among hundreds who have written me, concerning what many call "the biggest mistake" of their lives, or sex change. I present this representative group of gut-wrenching personal testimonials to put the transgender advocates on notice: we survivors know there is deep trouble in Trans La La Land.

I wrote this book because I want others to catch a glimpse of the raw emotions and experiences of people who are harmed by the grand—and dangerous—experiment of cross-sex hormones and surgical affirming procedures. You will see why these good people wish they had never surrendered the one life they have to the transgender ideology and why they now want to undo the damage done to their bodies. The advocates misled them, and when regret sets in, the advocates abandon them to their pain.

I found encouragement to go public with my story of sex change regret through the writings of Dr. Paul McHugh of Johns Hopkins University Hospital, who many years ago started challenging the transgender ideology. What Dr. McHugh wrote about psychology, not biology, driving the desire to change genders rang true to me because of my own experience and inspired me to write my autobiography, *A Transgender's Faith*.

I wondered if there were more like me. My wife and I launched our website, SexChangeRegret.com, to reach out and find others. Individuals with gender distress and transition regret contacted me and I talked with so many whom the medical solution of cross-sex hormones and sex-change surgery had failed and caused greater harm. Oh yes, there are more like me; too many.

In 2015, driven to expose that regret is real, and through the recommendation of my good friend, Stella Morabito, I began writing articles for TheFederalist.com, ThePublicDiscourse.com and DailySignal.com and today I have over fifty articles published. (I'm very fortunate that my wife is skilled in editing what I write. I can tell you none of my writings would have been published or had the worldwide impact they do without my wife or the good people who publish them. To all, I extend my most profound "Thank you.")

In this book the names of those who wrote the emails are kept private, with names changed and identifying details erased, lest their hurt be worsened by attacks from those who are still true believers in gender change. What is important is the suffering, heartache, abuse, deep loss and trauma they all share. We see through their words how life events caused them to want to escape into an alternate identity as a different gender and different person. Sometime later, after pursuing an elaborate gender transition using hormones and surgeries, they all found that changing gender was a folly, a temporary reprieve, not a lifelong solution to their pain or disorders.

The emails vividly display the emotions, confusion and questions that accompany the desire to go back. These emotional snapshots condemn the scientific endeavor that has put so many people at war with their sex.

The failure of gender-affirming hormones and surgical procedures to resolve gender distress rests squarely on the backs of advocates who stand in the way of providing good, sound, effective psychotherapy for these suffering people. In all the cases I see, each person incorrectly and unnecessarily identifies as being the opposite gender.

As you read through these stories, you'll see the need for more stringent standards of care for the gender distressed that focus on gaining psychological and emotional wellbeing, rather than fast-tracking people to undergo irreversible surgical procedures.

By giving light to the stories from survivors, others with gender dysphoria may back away from unnecessary surgery or for those who went through gender transition and want to go back, they will find comfort knowing they aren't the only one.

Perhaps, if we dare to dream big, the groups who ostracize and persecute these precious people will finally treat them with compassion and love and allow them to get the treatment they deserve to have.

The survivors live quietly with shattered dreams and altered bodies. Sometimes, hope is entirely lost, and suicide seems like the only option to end the suffering.

Like a prosecutor in a courtroom, this book provides first-hand testimony, expert witnesses and evidence that sex change procedures fail to provide the promised relief over the long term. Dr. Ihlenfeld, who was an endocrinologist in the 1970s administering cross-sex hormones in Harry Benjamin's gender clinic, said, "There is too much unhappiness among those who had surgery." The doctor was right, and you will read emails from people that show he is still right half a century later, starting first with Billy's story.

> *Note: If you have any questions about transgender terms used in this book, please refer to the glossary in the back.*

PART 1

Emails *and* Stories

1 Billy, a Small Skinny Boy with a Speech Impediment[1]

Billy remembers, as a young child, being curious about the differences between boys and girls, between him and his sister. In the first grade, as he looked around his classroom, he wondered where he belonged: with the boys or with the girls? Billy says his body told him he belonged with the boys, but his thoughts were telling him he belonged with the girls.

He had been dressing up as a girl at home, putting on his sister's makeup and earrings out of curiosity mostly. This can be a benign behavior that children grow out of, but in some situations, it can evolve into an escape into a fantasy world.

Being a small skinny boy with a speech impediment, the other children often teased him. They would taunt him, saying "What did you say?" and "I can't understand you" when he would try to speak. Billy was too physically small and verbally challenged to fight back, so he swallowed his emotions and withdrew.

---

[1] This first appeared as an article in Public Discourse: Ethics, Law, and the Common Good, the online journal of the Witherspoon Institute of Princeton, NJ, and is reprinted here with permission.
Heyer, W., "Childhood Sexual Abuse, Gender Dysphoria, and Transition Regret: Billy's Story," *Public Discourse*, March 26th, 2018, accessed on May 5, 2018, http://www.thepublicdiscourse.com/2018/03/21178/

Billy did not like his skinny body or speech difficulty. Nightly he prayed, begging God to change him into a girl so that the other kids wouldn't make fun of him. But his prayers seemed answered with something even worse: sex abuse.

Abuse, shame, and pain

In the summer after sixth grade, Billy's world came crashing down. At summer swimming league, Billy's new diving instructor targeted Billy for sexual abuse—abusers have a knack for picking on the weakest kids. Billy says, "The coach played with me." In other words, the diving coach perpetrated a horrific crime against a vulnerable child.

Billy was so traumatized he did not tell anyone for a very long time. Billy pushed the emotions away with strenuous physical activity—bicycling, swimming, and running. Billy says he would do this "until the pain in my body was greater than the pain in my mind." He also escaped by using his sister's makeup and earrings. He says that after the sexual abuse "I so very much hated my appendage"—that is, his male genitalia.

Billy is not the first who turned to a transgender identity to escape pain and trauma. In fact, Billy's story is not all that different than my own. And tragically, this story is repeated by so many other regretful people who attempted transition: childhood sexual abuse abounds.

The shame and pain of being used by a sexual predator is beyond the imagination. Most abused kids push the feelings deep inside and shut out the memories. The pain, shame, guilt, and fear often keep them from telling anyone about the abuse until much later in life, if they ever do. Many sexual abuse victims—like Billy, me, and others who write to me—get swept up by gender activist therapists who suggest that the proper treatment is to start on powerful sex hormones followed by gender "affirming" surgery. The problem is that hormones and surgery will not be effective in providing long-term treatment for depression or other ailments caused by sexual trauma.

Too many therapists rush to prescribe radical hormonal and surgical measures before diagnosing and treating the psychiatric disorders shown to coexist in the majority of gender dysphoric clients: depression, phobias, and adjustment disorders.[2] Billy's story illustrates the importance of digging into why a person wants to surgically alter his or her body and not simply accepting the idea that crossdressing or role-playing as the opposite sex means that children need a sex change.

Like many men who identify as women and want their genitalia surgically removed, Billy was still attracted to women.

In college, he fell in love with a woman, and the intensity of the feelings blew the hinges off the doors that had locked his emotions up inside him. Overwhelmed, he asked his sister for advice, and she helped him find a sexuality therapist. Billy says, "I spent the first of many years trying to find out why I was this way."

Unraveling the how and why of behavior shaped by traumatic events is never quick or easy work, especially early in the process. Billy told his therapist about the sexual abuse, the therapist instead focused on Billy's feeling like a female. Billy read all the books he could find on the topic, and he became convinced that once he transitioned all would be okay. Affirmed by his therapists and confident in knowing what he had to do, he decided to

---

[2] Azadeh Mazaheri Meybodi, Ahmad Hajebi, and Atefeh Ghanbari Jolfaei, "Psychiatric Axis I Comorbidities among Patients with Gender Dysphoria," *Psychiatry Journal*, vol. 2014, Article ID 971814, 5 pages, 2014, accessed on May 22, 2018, https://doi.org/10.1155/2014/971814.

surgically alter his male genitalia to a facsimile of a female's.

Billy's therapist referred him to a doctor in New Orleans who would provide hormone therapy to start the transition. Then came feminizing cosmetic and genital surgeries, dieting to lose muscle mass, and changing his name from Billy to Billie. He kept his employment, but it was not an easy transition. Billie had a high-flying career as an engineer.

But, in Billy's words, "All of the effort, pain and expense was for naught." After living seven to eight years as a female, Billy started attending church. As he grew in his faith in God, he realized his trans-life was a lie he could not live any longer. Billy started thinking in earnest about detransitioning back to the man God had originally intended him to be.

Billie successfully detransitioned back to Billy and met a beautiful lady who had two daughters from a previous marriage. They became friends, fell in love and got married in 2011.

Billy says, "I do have problems, but it's my choice of living a happy and productive life or let my problems get the best of me." Billy says he has chosen to get his strength, comfort, and forgiveness from God through Jesus Christ and live with joy.

Billy's story is among the first of many stories—including my own—where gender confusion is rooted in childhood sex abuse.

Another commonality is the raw emotion they are experiencing. The next person expresses the complexity of emotion and the heart longings of someone who wishes they hadn't had surgery.

2 Kevin, "The biggest mistake of my life"

As Kevin told me, face-to-face just a few months ago, sex change surgery was "the biggest mistake of my life." Kevin is a trans-woman at a crossroads. He has been living as a female for 12 years, has a great career, but wants to move out of the trans madness and back to living as a male. Recently, he shared his turbulent feelings with me in an email:

> *Walt,*
>
> *You know how difficult this can be and there are times when the weight of it all literally brings me to my knees. My heart is heavy, the journey long, the pain I feel is real. I never thought I'd say this, but I need hope because all too often I feel a sense of hopelessness. I feel abandoned, ostracized, outcast and alone. When hope is gone you are left with two things; perseverance and faith. It is not much, and I know this because I am there.*
>
> *I long to be like Billy [the detransitioner from the previous story], to find love again, to live again. I sense his joy. It gives me hope that there are people out there who, despite my own failings could still desire me. I am on a mission to find that special person in my life who will love me for all I am. Who will believe in me, who I can share the joys and*

sorrows with, who will strengthen me and help me live a life pleasing to God.

Thank you, Walt for inspiring me, for sharing; for offering friendship and support, prayers and guidance when so many others have not.

In closing I just want to give you this important update: I met with my pastor and told him of my plans to return to life as a man. He offered his support and shared that it was his belief that God was calling me to do this. If God is with me, Walt, I cannot fail.

Kevin

3 Blair, Guinness World Record Holder

If anyone ever went the distance in pursuing their gender perception, Blair did: 167 surgeries in 18 years from 1987 to 2005 in his quest to resolve gender dysphoria with surgery. He won the Guinness World Record for the most gender-reassignment surgeries for an individual person but lost the battle to find his "authentic" gender. Indeed, judging by the sheer number of surgeries they performed, the surgeons demonstrated a blatant disregard for Blair's physical and emotional wellbeing.

Candidates for sex change surgeries are vulnerable and ill-equipped to grasp the consequences of surgeries on their bodies and the effects on their future. They are easily approved for unnecessary procedures by surgeons willing to accommodate them.

Blair's story[3] is a cautionary tale for anyone today who is considering the use of cross-sex hormones and gender-change surgery to feel better about themselves. The

---

[3] Blair's story first appeared in *The Daily Signal* and has been edited for inclusion here. Reprinted with permission.
Heyer, W., "This Man Received 167 Sex-Change Surgeries. He Lives in a World of Regret.", *The Daily Signal*, January 12, 2018, accessed on May 6, 2018, https://www.dailysignal.com/2018/01/12/man-received-167-sex-change-surgeries-lives-world-regret/

mainstream media and the transgender health community blithely claim that rigorous requirements are in place to prevent sex change regret. But this story illustrates how unevenly applied the standards are and that surgical predators exist to take advantage of vulnerable people. And it calls into question whether the standards are even valid.

On a cold, snowy December morning in a Maryland coffee shop, Blair shared his story with me. In 1987, at the age of 26, Blair underwent the first of many cosmetic surgeries to change his gender/sex appearance from male to trans-female. Within a few months, he said he deeply regretted becoming a trans-woman.

For the next five years, he struggled in his life as a woman before undergoing another genital surgical change to restore his original male self. But peace with his gender eluded him.

With gender dysphoria still present and feeling unsettled, Blair for a second time was approved and underwent yet another gender change, once more self-identifying as trans-female.

But the distress persisted, as did Blair: more feminizing surgeries followed as doctors indulged his requests for more. More surgeries only brought more regret. Blair was caught in a cycle of surgery-offers-hope; then surgery-brings-disappointment or worse, despair.

By 2005, seven cosmetic surgeons had performed 167 gender-affirming surgeries on his body, filling their bank accounts to the tune of more than $220,000 and leaving him, in his words, "disfigured."

Some who contact me regret their one surgery. Blair regrets every one of his 167 surgeries. Having painfully proven that surgeons cannot construct his "true self," Blair found his true male self in following Jesus Christ.

The doctors and surgeons failed him in their responsibility to "first, do no harm"—as the Hippocratic

Oath says—while profiting from the 167 disfiguring surgeries. Yet, they will not be held accountable or responsible for gross medical misconduct or malpractice against this good man.

At some point, these surgeons should have refused requests for more surgery and protected Blair from harming himself further. Instead, they sold their surgeries to him despite his emotionally, psychologically, and sexually unhealthy and unstable psyche.

4 Rick to Rachael in 15 Months

This young man's body is permanently damaged because doctors, who have no definitive idea as to who will persist in a condition of gender dysphoria (more on that subject in the children's section), propose irreversible treatments for young people who feel conflicted about gender. But as Rick found out, strongly held feelings can be seen in retrospect as "failed thinking."

> *I wish someone would have been brutally honest with me*

> *The whole gender reassignment approval process is completely out of control. I did the whole thing in 15 months and was not required by the surgeon to live out a real-life transition prior to the surgical procedure—truly misguided!*
>
> *I agree with you, especially among the older transgender group—regret must be much higher because the quoted rate of attempted suicide is rampant.*
>
> *Our message must get out—approval requirements must be so stringent as to be prohibitive (especially for older people with normal native anatomy and chromosomes).*
>
> *I wish someone would have been brutally honest with me and shown me that I had failed thinking*

and that I would never be more than an amusement to others.

What a devastating result for Rick. You might dismiss this as an exception; that fast-tracking a deeply troubled patient to such a life-altering (and damaging) decision within barely a year is an outlier. But in fact, it gets even worse, as I learned from the next story—where surgery came just a single month after he sought help.

5 Sam Referred for Surgery After 30 Days

Sam lived in pain, and that pain lived in him for so long that he was desperate for relief.

I have severe PTSD from "transition"

He sought out a psychologist who, after meeting with him for one month, recommended that he have surgery on his genitalia. Her professional opinion was that Sam "had been born into the wrong body and should really have been female."

Sam was fast-tracked to surgery even though the reason he sought counseling was for psychotic depression and childhood sexual abuse. Result? More pain, more depression, more panic attacks, and worst of all, thoughts of ending it all by suicide.

I presented as a female in September 2008 for psychological help and therapy following a series of difficult and traumatic life events which caused both childhood sexual abuse and psychotic depression to return to the forefront. She met with me for a month and had me see a psychiatrist in October 2008. I assumed [I was seeing a psychiatrist] to get psychiatric medication. Instead, I discovered that the psychiatrist and therapist had jointly agreed that the real cause of my problems was that I had been born into the wrong body and should really have been female.

I have always been androgynous (and in fact, suffer from the real chemical condition known as Androgen Insensitivity Syndrome) and never fully developed in puberty secondary sex male characteristics.

Anyways, I was referred to a urologist of their choosing in November 2008. My surgery was scheduled in March 2009 and so less than 4 months later, without a real-life test, without being on hormones - all they did was make me take Finasteride to shut down any possible testosterone activity - and then, in the middle of March 2009 they had me chopped and mutilated.

And yes, I know, I should have gone running or gotten a lawyer or moved but honestly, I wanted the answer to be so simple and wanted to believe them that soon, I would be my true self and my problems would go away. I had lived in so much pain for so long that I was desperate and also prone to depressive and delusional states.

So, I had the "unnecessary genitalia surgery" in March 2009 and in April 2009, with the urologist's letter, legally "became female" and began taking Estradiol maintenance. Yes, you are reading that right, they waited until after "the surgery" to give me female hormones. So then, I rested and waited to feel better thinking it was just post-operative pain.

In August 2009 I underwent a neuropsychological evaluation which stated that I had severe self-esteem issues and also had a deficit in reality testing.

I kept just trying to go to bed and rest, kept thinking it was all an issue of time needed for physical healing. After all, that is one heck of a surgery. This turned into me essentially staying in bed and doing nothing for the better part of year.

I was so depressed! It wasn't until March 2010 that I tried to start taking walks around town but ended up having severe panic attacks. These panic attacks got worse and climaxed in May 2010 where I ended up visiting an ER for chest pains. By August 2010 I was acutely suicidal and came very near to ending my own life, were it not for my wife, I would have.

Also, by this time, my appearance had changed to the point where everyone thought I was female and if I said otherwise, even doctors, even OB/GYNs didn't believe me.

In November 2010, I had a complete psychotic break and ended up being shuffled around from hospital to hospital until April 2011. I was put on different antipsychotics and was even diagnosed with Schizophrenia. Finally, I was drugged up enough that I shut up and stopped trying to tell people what happened to me and I went home.

My wife and I moved out of the area and into a predominantly Catholic community in a different part of the state and have attempted to find a way to move on and rebuild life. Oh yes, and I go to therapy every week, but now I see a Catholic therapist, who agrees with me that in addition to whatever else was the case, I have severe PTSD from "transition" and from them butchering my postoperative medical and mental health.

It is only now that my mind has had a chance for partial recovery and reintegration that I am able to start looking into what a detransition path looks like. Neither my physical or mental health is going to improve further until I find a way to fix my hormonal situation.

Sam's story is egregious, and even more so when you see the same themes repeated: Childhood sex abuse and depression. Supposedly competent psychologists, psychiatrists and surgeons went to work on Sam but, rather than deal with the agonizing list of ills, they pumped this terribly vulnerable man full of hormones and whittled at him with the knife. Yet even once he looked so female as to fool other doctors, his pain remained, and worsened. Hope came only when he met counselors who spoke of integrating his mind with the reality of his male body. One wonders how Sam might have healed had that been the first answer to his suffering, instead of the last.

6 Michael's Suicidal 18 Months After Surgery

In 2004 the UK University of Birmingham reported that some people after a sex change remain traumatized to the point of suicide.[4] That academic report took on flesh and blood when this man's email showed up in my inbox.

Michael's story is typical of the people who write me for help: emotionally traumatic

I have to pray for the strength not to go to the gun store. Every minute is filled with suicidal thoughts.
I can't live like this anymore. Please help me.

childhood events led to the desire for gender change, but after the surgery, the emotional issues remained, waiting to be addressed.

Just 18 months after sex change surgery, Michael deeply regretted his surgical sex change and was distressed to the point of suicide. But he found hope in my story as he walked through this most difficult time with the help of a licensed counselor—fortunately a counselor who was independent of the gender change machine.

---

[4] Batty, D., Sex changes are not effective, say researchers, *The Guardian*, 30 Jul 2004, accessed on August 14, 2018 at
http://www.theguardian.com/society/2004/jul/30/health.mentalhealth

One email became another, then another, until we'd corresponded some 250 times in a year. Here are some excerpts.

> *I am 46 and 1.5 years post op male to female I struggled with my gender identity most of my life. I am so miserable and every day after the reassignment surgery I struggle to get thru the next minute. I have to pray for the strength not to go to the gun store. Every minute is filled with suicidal thoughts. I can't live like this anymore. Please help me. Guide me what to do medically, surgically to fix this mess.*
>
> *Please help me*
> *Michael*

Please help me? It is a fearful thing to suddenly become a lifeline to such a troubled soul. So, I gently probed, and within a dozen hours Michael revealed that his surgery was driven by a misdiagnosis of gender dysphoria. The error was terrible, as he discovered when he met with a new therapist shortly after the surgery. What bedeviled this man was not gender dysphoria but a transvestic fetish, which is extreme, sexually-driven crossdressing. He was never distressed with his gender identity and he didn't benefit from sex change surgery.

Michael's emotions were laid bare as he told his story. He asked the question that none of those doctors would ever answer: Why couldn't this have been discovered before surgery?

> *Hi Walt,*
> *I am so glad I came across your website. After 10 months of post-op psychotherapy, I know sadly now my problems were great depression, unresolved issues as you said (I was sexually abused by my*

grandfather at 3 years old, father was killed in the Air Force when I was 5, grew up thinking I must be gay, had sex with men and was disgusted, and cross dressed most of my life.) My new therapist is calling it a Transvestic Fetish that went terribly wrong, coupled with GID [Gender Identity Disorder]. Why we couldn't get to this pre-op? It's just a sick money-making industry as I see it.

I have already removed the breast implants and will be restarting testosterone soon. I have destroyed my career, my finances, my marriage and alienated my family. The pain as you know is so great! It feels like a knife in my heart. I can't sleep, I pace the house looking in my shorts for my manhood. I am so disgusted with myself. How could a smart, successful guy get so lost? I had it all. Now I'm watching it slowly fade away.

You and all the people that give me words of encouragement are the only thing keeping me going. I have rope, and I know when and where all the next gun shows are; I don't want to live like this. My therapist is going to recommend me to gender therapists; to get a surgical solution I can live with. At 46, I don't want all those forearm, body scars. I just hope I have the strength to get there; my batteries are drained. I have not read your book; but, I am willing to listen to your thoughts and ideas. Have a good day. Thank you.

Once more we see the telling data point: this man was sexually abused by his grandfather at age 3. Later that same day, Michael wrote about the consequences he bears in his body:

I realize if I get a phalloplasty [addition of a penis] it will not be the original equipment. I just don't want to look at this. I think a vaginal closure and a meta with testicle implants will at least help my mind. It's just like a "bad dream" and it won't go away. You can think you're a woman, you can fantasize and dress like a woman; but, you will never be a woman. No, the sex change surgery did not change my gender/sex either. It just made every second of my day unbearable and a living hell.

With each subsequent email, he revealed more about his sex change journey. He told how he got caught up in the transgender community in Thailand and had his surgery there. Now he wishes he had been required to have therapy for childhood issues before getting the surgery. As he says, "A 'sick' man can't make 'well' decisions, can he?"

Hi My Friend,

I was thinking yesterday that I'm in a select group of people right now and soon I will enter an even more select group by attempting to surgically return back to my birth gender. For me, Walt, nothing less will suffice.

The other day after our session, my therapist said, "you are cutting-edge." I guess I must explain exactly what he means by that; and why everyone is so surprised I am even still alive. Yes, my story is filled with the same childhood sexual abuse, abandonment, a lifetime of cross dressing, homosexual activities, alcoholism and cross gender fantasies, etc. The usual stuff!

But, that's where my story stops and gets a little different. You see, Walt, I was living and working in Shenzhen, China. Bangkok was only a three-hour flight from Hong Kong. I spent every holiday in Thailand. I was very comfortable among the ladyboys, kathoey. They accepted me as one of their own and I had made many friends there.

The Thai surgeons certainly didn't ask me had I had therapy, tell me or suggest I get therapy before making this decision. In my sick twisted mind of the time; I had made the decision. The mirror saw a woman looking back asking; "Are you sure you want to do this?" I was asked. Well Walt, a "sick" man can't make "well" decisions, can he? The rest is history and the tragedy that unfolded.

And that is why my story is so intriguing to the U.S. mental health community. What happened to me is about to happen on a much grander scale right here in the U.S and the rest of the "civilized world." If you have read the WPATH SOC version 7[5], it has literally removed the gatekeepers, Real Life Test, and timeline for hormones and surgery. And knowing how I got here, I know it's not going to be good for them as well.

No matter how we got here—whether standards were followed, intentionally bypassed or the person was as deluded and ignorant as myself—how to stop others from making the same disastrous decisions is more important.

The problem is, as you know, when this disgusting thing consumes your life, you're not open to hearing the "truth." All I saw was the websites, videos and "girls" in the streets of Bangkok telling me how "pretty" I was going to be. In hindsight, we know how delusional that idea was!

---

[5] The World Professional Association for Transgender Health (WPATH) develops guidelines for the treatment of people having discomfort with their gender identity, called the standards of care for transgender health, now in the seventh revision (SOC-7).

You would think that as Michael finally recognized how the false reality he sought was doing nothing but harm, then his therapist would join him on this healing journey. But no—not when the therapist has bought into gender identity theory:

> *Walt. This morning the "pro-transsexual" county supported (sliding scale) therapist that I have been working with for 9/10 months just told me she couldn't work with me any longer.*
>
> *I told her "Of course not, I don't fit into your LGBT mission statement. If I wanted a vagina you would facilitate that. But, if I say I made a mistake, help me fix this, you can't help me."*
>
> *I am at a loss. I can't afford a psychologist at the "real rate." That leaves me either a man with a vagina or a woman by default. That's where I am at right now. Aggravated with myself!*
>
> *Michael*

I cannot put it any better than he did: a "sick" man can't make "well" decisions, can he? But even as Michael fought his way to wellness—in a battle where his therapist was the enemy—making the "well" decision real is daunting. It is no small surgery to restore refashioned body parts to appear as they did originally. It would be so much better to receive good, effective psychotherapy to avoid sex change surgery and all the body-change mess, rather than suffer this international tale of surgery and sorrow.

7 The Turmoil of Transition and Detransition

People who opt for gender transition are blissfully unaware of the many difficulties involved. After all, they are cheered onward with a chorus from gender medical experts and the community of trans activists: "Surgery will make me real!" Forward they go, full of hope and anticipation of an improved life. But gender transition is a difficult process for most people on many levels:

- Emotionally, they withstand and cope with the various reactions of friends, family and employers as they reveal and defend their decision.

- Physically, they undergo numerous gender-changing surgeries and procedures, each accompanied by pain and recovery.

- Legally, they change their name and gender on all identity documents.

- Socially and mentally, they often change wardrobe, hair style, pronouns and name and adjust to living in an unfamiliar gender.

All these significant milestones require tremendous energy, drive and commitment to achieve. When completed, the changes add up to a new life built on a new identity.

But as I've learned hundreds of times over, that new identity is dogged by old problems. Their expectations unmet, they are suddenly all alone in a difficult place. They haven't really changed gender, but they have built a completely new life as if they had.

Walking back from that decision requires admitting that building a life on a different gender wasn't the long-term solution. It means finding caring, psychological counseling to discover what drove them to undergo such a drastic transformation. Then, when ready, they need to muster the courage to undo the transition steps to achieve detransition.

That's one reason—maybe "the" reason—I went online with my story: I hoped that in telling my story, some who felt alone with regret would be inspired to seek the restoration of being their true sex.

In the next several emails, vulnerable people express questions and concerns relating specifically to detransition.

8 Teresa Terrified of Detransition to Tyler

In contrast to their previous naiveté, people who want to go back to their birth gender are fully aware of the challenges and difficulties of the process. Not having the starry-eyed wonder or the support of the trans community that carried them through the first time, the return trip seems unbelievably daunting. One of the first steps is to reach out and find someone who will listen.

> *Subject: Transgender Regret*
> *Hi. I'm beginning to feel like I'm a man again. I'm terrified of going through a detransitioning.*
> *Transitioning was very hard... Do you have any advice on how I might go about it?*
> *Thanks. Teresa [wants to be Tyler again]*

In subsequent emails, Teresa and I discussed the medical, social and legal aspects of detransitioning. I assured her that even though detransitioning is hard, it is worth it.

9 Austin/Andrea Age 27 Considers Reversal

The next person's story is painfully common. Even though she sees herself as a successful MTF transition, she's thinking

I've been considering reversal recently, but I'm afraid of so many things.

about detransitioning. But she's afraid, embarrassed, overwhelmed, and can't find resources to help her through the process.

I saw your YouTube videos and I'm curious how you managed to live as a man again. I am considering a similar route.

I transitioned pretty young and I'm 27 now. I had SRS at 21 and been living as female/a feminine guy for some years before that.

I've been considering reversal recently, but I'm afraid of so many things…There's so many things to consider and the whole list makes my head hurt at times.

I would say I'm a pretty successful transition story - since I'm physically attractive, have a good career and a good social circle, so I'd be pretty embarrassed that I'm considering all this.

I have spoken to my father lately, and he seems encouraging and willing to help me out on this path.

But the resources that I require to help me along the way seem really scarce.
Andrea (Austin)

Scarce, indeed! When I started my outreach, often it seemed like I was alone. And too often, I still feel that way. Yet slowly the resource base has grown, as loving and caring people have questioned the claims of gender ideology. (Some of the websites I've found helpful are listed ' in the appendix.)

Interesting how even people like Andrea who appear to be the epitome of a transition success story—physically attractive, good career, robust social circle—consider reversal after living the trans life for years.

10 Mr. M's Concerns

So far, I've related the trials of men who thought themselves female. But women suffer similar challenges, seeking to solve their life problems by proclaiming themselves to be male. This is one such story, and like most people who contact me full of regret about changing genders, Mr. M (born Michelle) doesn't want anyone to know.

> *Hi Walt, I am a female-to-male transsexual who had a hysterectomy and mastectomy and now I regret it because, although I pass, I feel like a fake.*
>
> *Do you think I'd have an easy time detransitioning?*
>
> *I know the trans community will hate me, but will my friends and the public see me as courageous?*
>
> *I look male from the chest up but female from the waist down with a female voice. I just don't think I'll pass flat-chested with a shadow. I don't want unsafe implants. I'd appreciate any thoughts.*
>
> *I'm trying to grow my hair and get electrolysis so that may help. Is electrolysis really that painful? Is it effective for everyone?*
>
> *Thanks,*
>
> *Mr. M (Michelle)*
>
> *Ps. I don't want anyone to know I'm contemplating going back.*

Total reversibility is not possible. Michelle is aware of some of the penalties she will endure from taking male hormones, such as shadow or beard growth. She will need electrolysis to remove the facial hair, and yes, it is painful and expensive. Other masculine effects, such as bulky muscle tone and sharpened facial features, will soften on their own over time. She's fortunate that her voice didn't deepen, and she still sounds female.

Surgical changes are permanent. The hysterectomy removed her uterus, so the option for biological children is gone forever. Double mastectomies left her flat-chested and with chest scars. Implanting fake breasts is an option for helping her appearance but surgery is painful and expensive. Thankfully, like most female-to-male transitioners, she didn't alter her genitalia and vagina, so they will function the same as they do now.

Living life knowing you're a fake is exhausting and I'm happy for Michelle that she's thinking of going back. But the detransition process is never easy, takes time and is punctuated with a lot of ups and downs. Regretters going back need people around them to lend strength for the journey—people willing to listen with love, speak healing words, provide emotional, legal and financial assistance, and cheer them on to their homecoming.

11 David to Donna at Age 23

This man started his transition to female at age 19 and had surgery at age 23. At that time, the doctors lined up to counsel, operate, and medicate. But now—silence from the medical profession. So once more, I find myself answering the typical—and painful—questions he asks about detransitioning his body to make it appear masculine again.

> *Walt,*
>
> *I was wondering if you had some advice for me about reverting to living as a man. I began transitioning at age 19 and had SRS [Sex Reassignment Surgery] at age 23. I tried to stick it out for years but after I reached age 28 or so I couldn't stand my facade any longer.*
>
> *I've been back on testosterone for years (I'm 35 now) but now I have small breasts (less than an A-cup) to consider and of course, having a neo-vagina instead of a penis.*
>
> *As far as I know, however, there is no reversal of the vaginoplasty surgery. Phalloplasty seems rudimentary at best.*

Vaginoplasty surgery is sex reassignment surgery on a biological male, where the surgeon refashions parts of the male testicles and penis into a female-appearing vagina, clitoris and labia flaps for sexual relations and evacuating urine. Because vaginoplasty originates from the male parts, reversal is impossible.

Phalloplasty, addition of an artificial penis, is intricate and expensive, and as David says, the results are rudimentary at best. The reconstructed penis can't naturally achieve erection, and organism may be a thing of the past. Most men don't bother, but for some, it's worth it for the psychological benefits of seeing something there and the ability to pee standing up.

Each day, as detransitioned men like David dress for the day, their physical scars and genital reconfiguration remind them of how they fell for the propaganda that glorifies reassignment surgery. The gender specialists declared, "Don't worry; regret is rare," but that assurance rings hollow now.

In my life, there was nothing more important than getting my life back. I found detransitioning challenging, yet essential. I had to persevere through it because my healing depended on it.

In the process of detransitioning, deciding on which masculinizing surgeries or medical procedures to have is not the most important issue. (In Part 3—Facts and Information, you'll find descriptions of common detransition procedures.) What matters is healing the emotional and psychological wounds of the past and living authentically and true to one's biological sex.

12 The Suicide of Kyle Scanlon, Trans Leader and Mentor

One of the audience members came to the open mike and asked the question I knew was coming: "What causes the high rate of suicide attempts in the trans population? Is it because society doesn't accept the trans person?"

The one-word answer to that is "no." But the more complete answer, reported on a Toronto news site, reveals further that even being an accepted, respected transman does not cure the underlying depression that can lead a person to take their life.

Kyle Scanlon of Toronto, Canada, lived the life that gender activists claim is essential if the gender dysphoric soul is to avoid succumbing to suicide. The only answer, they say, is swift and absolute gender affirmation.

Kyle, who transitioned from female to male, was well-known and well-respected, very much a valued leader and mentor in the Toronto trans community. Not only a role model as a transman, Kyle coordinated the education, training, and research efforts at the 519 Community Centre in Toronto and was committed to improving the quality of life in the trans community.

Kyle died July 3, 2012 by suicide.

Despite Kyle's full-bore transition, Kyle's friends said he suffered from untreated depression before and even after his transition to living as a man.[6] Kyle's close friend, Janet Knights, who knew of those struggles, said that Kyle "had many friends and acquaintances and did find peace with his family. But it wasn't enough. It could never be enough."

Blaming society for Kyle's death is convenient to the trans activist narrative used to lobby for legislation, but clearly it was the depression Kyle suffered which was not effectively treated that eventually led to suicide. Kyle died at his own hand because the transgender activists refuse to acknowledge the problem of depression in the trans community or that gender transition is not effective or proper treatment for depression.

Suicide.org says untreated depression is the leading cause of suicide, but this reality is consistently set aside when someone tells their doctor that they dislike their birth sex and hate their bodies. Suddenly, the focus is not saving a life from depression, but driving that soul toward gender transition at all costs—even, tragically, when the cost is the death of a patient.

Kyle, at the very center of a very supportive transgender community that was replete with support and approval for living and being a transgender male, still chose death. That should be a lesson for us all. You can blame "society," but it's the untreated comorbid mental disorders, like depression, which trigger the staggering number of transgender suicides.

Such are the fruits when doctors recklessly drive adults toward a sex change. And for children and adolescents, it's even more dangerous. The influential

---

[6] Demchuk, D., Toronto's Trans Community Grieves Loss of Kyle Scanlon: Community leader paved way for trans acceptance and understanding., *Torontoist*, July 10, 2012, accessed on May 23, 2018, https://torontoist.com/2012/07/toronto%E2%80%99s-trans-community-grieves-loss-of-kyle-scanlon/

adults in their lives—parents, teachers, doctors, school boards—affirm the child's chosen gender rather than the birth sex. The affirmation and acceptance from trusted adults inflict excessive psychological and emotional pressure on far-from-mature, gender-questioning kids.

The suicides continue because doctors fail to effectively diagnose and treat the comorbid mental disorders. Scanlon's suicide is the factual evidence, an unfortunate consequence of focusing on the outward appearance when psychological issues run deep inside. Some day we will learn what Scanlon's friend wisely perceived: that no amount of change—including all the surgeries to "look good"—can ever be enough to heal the ache inside. How long will it take before the gender affirmation doctors recognize the basic truth: a "sick" man can't make "well" decisions, can he?

13 The Suicide of Blake Brockington, First Openly Trans Homecoming King

No one seems to see that transgender individuals live on the edge of suicide because of untreated depression. Instead, everyone wants to ignore the person's mental state,

But those close to him also knew Brockington was struggling — with his transition and other issues

which drives suicidal thoughts, and instead blame the tragedy on rejection from society, community, school, church, friends and family. But, as this story shows, treating depression is far more important than encouraging, supporting and advocating for a change of gender. Depression can be deadly.

In this story taken from the headlines[7], female-to-male high school senior Blake Brockington gained fame as the first openly transgender homecoming king at East Mecklenburg High School near Charlotte, NC, in 2014. Less than a year after the high school graduation, he was

---

[7] Garloch, K., "Charlotte-area transgender teens' suicides rock community", *The Charlotte Observer*, March 28, 2015, accessed on May 29, 2018, http://www.charlotteobserver.com/news/local/article16655111.html

on medical leave from his university studies. That leave ended tragically when Blake walked into oncoming traffic.

Brockington, born female, came out as trans in his sophomore year of high school, and sometime later started taking testosterone. His parents didn't understand or support his transition, so he was placed in foster care with a family that did. Brockington had close friends who describe him as vibrant and bright. He mentored younger trans children and youth at school. He ran track and was drum major with the band.

But Brockington had also been hospitalized for cutting. At a Trans Faith in Action Conference in Charlotte he told a group of attendees, including the pastor who later led his memorial service, that he wasn't sure if he wanted to continue to live or not.

> "From the outside, Brockington exuded a sense of confidence and strength, many have said in the past week. But those close to him also knew Brockington was struggling — with his transition and other issues."[8]

Brockington sought and received support from Time Out Youth Center, a local LGBT youth services agency. After graduation from high school, he became an outspoken advocate, speaking at transgender events and organizing public rallies.

It's clear that Brockington's troubles started early and never let up, even though he received everything the advocates say will prevent suicide:

- His friends accepted him and loved him.

---

[8] Comer, M., "Memorial remembers a 'larger than life' Blake Brockington", March 30, 2015, *Qnotes*, accessed on May 29, 2018, https://goqnotes.com/34808/memorial- remembers-a-larger-than-life-blake-brockington/

- His loving foster family supported his transition.

- His school supported his transition; he was even celebrated as homecoming king.

- A local LGBT youth services agency actively supported him.

- He had a supportive gender counselor.

But with all the focus on affirming Brockington's claimed gender, nobody dealt with the issues that drive people toward suicide. According to the National Alliance on Mental Illness (NAMI), suicide comes 90% of the time from mental illness such as depression, bipolar disorder or some other diagnosis.[9] Social or legal efforts to affirm gender are not directed at resolving depression; only sound diagnosis and treatment that *targets* the depression can hope to be effective in the prevention of suicide.

This sad story has been repeated and reported, name after name in obituaries, for years. Untreated mental disorders have plagued the transgender community, stealing life after life. The explanations that blame lack of acceptance and support are wearing thin.

Gender change advocates will argue, as they have, that transgender kids are vulnerable to social stigmatizing, and that's the reason for the suicides. But that is a smokescreen that relies on a flawed premise.

Suicide cannot always be averted. But by focusing only on propelling the person toward gender transition and failing to look for, and address, any accompanying mental disorders, transgender health providers are harming the very population they claim to help.

---

[9] Pappas, S., "Suicide: Statistics, Warning Signs and Prevention", *Live Science*, August 10, 2017, accessed on May 29. 2018, https://www.livescience.com/44615-suicide-help.html

14 Crossdressers Don't Need Surgery

Crossdressers can get caught up in the transgender whirlwind and mistakenly be diagnosed with gender dysphoria and treated with gender change surgery, to their harm and regret. It's important for medical practitioners to differentiate among the various disorders that present as gender dysphoria, such as transvestic disorder and autogynephilia.

When dressing as the opposite gender becomes the way to become sexually aroused, it is called transvestic *behavior*. When the crossdressing behavior becomes problematic in a person's life, it is then considered a transvestic *disorder*.

Psychology Today describes transvestic disorder and its expression and effects this way:

> "To be diagnosed with transvestic disorder, a person must experience persistent and intense sexual arousal from fantasizing about, or acting on, urges to wear one or more pieces of clothing normally worn by the opposite gender...
>
> Someone with transvestic disorder suffers anxiety, depression, guilt, or shame because of their urge toward crossdressing...

The feelings of distress over crossdressing that characterize transvestic disorder are separate and distinct from gender dysphoria."[10]

Autogynephilia is another, slightly different disorder in which a male derives sexual pleasure from fantasizing about himself as a woman. Just like someone with transvestic disorder, a male suffering from autogynephilia can be misdiagnosed as gender dysphoric and wrongly encouraged to change gender.

Having a lifelong wish to be a girl or a lifetime of obsessively crossdressing does not mean that gender change is needed or appropriate, as the next several emails illustrate quite well.

---

[10] https://www.psychologytoday.com/us/conditions/transvestic-disorder, accessed on May 23, 2018

15 Nathan Encounters God

Disordered thoughts about one's sex/gender can start from the smallest childish misconception and evolve into gender dysphoria.

Nathan, a British man who transitioned to Natalie, shares how something as simple as having a new baby sister, loneliness and harsh words from his father, can cause a five-year-old boy to feel unimportant and begin crossdressing as an escape. Subsequent life trauma can cause crossdressing to turn into a desire for gender transition.

This story also illustrates how powerful an impact an encounter with God can be, how truth brings clarity and liberation from transgender philosophy and that detransition is indeed possible.

> *Walt,*
>
> *I cross dressed from an early age, it was my way of escape. I would wear my mum's dresses and even pinched (took) clothes from the girl next door, who was five years older than me.*
>
> *Five years after I was born my parents had a baby girl and she became the center of my dad and mum's world. I felt that I had been forgotten. If I had been born a girl, I would be getting much more attention. My mum would go out and about with my sister, leaving me at home with the family dog. My*

father was a hardworking man. Setting up his own company, he tended to work seven days a week. I became a bit lonely in my own company. My dad would say things like, "Why do you sit like a girl" and he would say "Maybe we picked the wrong baby". Then the words that hurt: "No son of mine would act like this". I was never manly enough for him.

This was the nineteen sixties. On TV we had Batman, and other programs where ordinary people had double lives and became superheroes. I discovered that pop-stars changed their names and ages at will. My cross dressing meant I could become another person. I didn't have to be lonely me, so my bedroom became my world.

Through the seventies, eighties and nineties I cross dressed as often as I could. I also married three times and had three sons. One went to heaven. The other two are alive although I do not have contact with them or my parents and sister as they choose not to have contact with me. My wives all knew I dressed, so it wasn't a guilty secret.

My last girlfriend's son died at the age of nineteen in 2003 having cancer. I am not sure why, but it hit me hard and our relationship ended. I felt I had failed as a man somehow. A few years before this another girlfriend had committed suicide and I found her dead in our bed when I came home after working a night-shift.

In 2004 having stumbled across articles about transsexual (TS) people, this seemed to fit me, and I went all out to change my life. I chatted with TS people online and learned the way to become a woman, at least that's what I thought. It took almost no time to be referred from my doctor to local psychiatrists, then on to Charring Cross Hospital

London, where it was confirmed I had gender dysphoria. I was on hormones and I transitioned while I worked full time for the National Health Service (NHS). I had many good and bad experiences while transitioning.

In 2008 I underwent sexual reassignment surgery. I was now taking six milligrams of estrogen, my bust was developing, also I had been having speech therapy and laser hair removal for my beard. I was convinced I was a woman.

The surgery was considered a success. I say this as after I returned home the depth of my vagina internal wall collapsed from six inches to about two inches. With the surgical problems I was devastated. I went back to the surgeon three months later, the channel opened again, the same results occurred. The surgeon told me he could not do anything more and I was discharged. It did not stop me however having two boyfriends and a relationship with another post-op TS over the next two years.

I became baptized. I had given my life to Jesus. I was so happy. I had everything I had ever wanted in life: God, good friends and living as a woman. [But] the next two months were the hardest I have ever been through.

I would wake up early in the morning and hear someone calling my name. I jumped out of bed and would look everywhere for this person.

I had many nightmares and dreams and this voice kept saying my name. Finally, one morning after another restless night, I was getting ready for work. Unbelievably, I was still shaving as I still had stubble and was about to apply my make up when I froze to the spot. I could see myself as if for the first time, a man looking back at me, not a woman.

I had this feeling inside me that Jesus was saying how much he loved me, and I was born a man and now was the time to change and become the man he had created. It was my choice.

I had this feeling deep down in me that God was right, and I was wrong. I packed up all my female clothes in one wardrobe, stopped wearing makeup and grew a beard. My female friend had taken a job working for a Christian rehab place. Her husband joined the male rehab. That is when I changed my name back to my male name, started testosterone injections once a month and completed nine months on the rehab I needed that time. I also went to church and have had many amazing experiences as a result.

I have since moved out of the rehab, now live in a shared house with friends. I have found a vibrant born-again church, Christian music and made many friends. Most of my work colleagues here, including my landlords, do not know about my past. I have only shared this with a few people, now with you.

God bless you.

Nathan

So many seem to edge toward gender change surgery—step by step they go (cross dressing, coming out, presenting as the opposite sex publicly, being socially affirmed, medicating with cross-sex hormones, pursuing feminizing or masculinizing surgeries) with each step seeming to help a bit, but not fixing the problem—not even after taking the giant leap past mutilating surgery. But there is a peculiar clarity at the point when they realize that they must revert.

16 Brian, Crossdresser, Spared Surgery

The following man did his research and realized his crossdressing was a fetish[11], not a case of gender dysphoria. That's an important distinction,

I thank you again for helping me to not make a life altering change that is irreversible.

because a person with a fetish desires to cross dress, not change gender.

Unfortunately, gender specialists often see everything as gender dysphoria and rapidly approve hormone therapies for crossdressers in total disregard for the long-term outcomes. It is a sad commentary on gender specialists when the person struggling, like this man Brian, must find the truth in a YouTube video and not in the doctor's office.

Walt,

I really appreciate you speaking about this issue. I have struggled for most of my life with gender identity issues, and often wish I were a girl.

---

[11] The Oxford Dictionary defines fetish as a "form of sexual desire linked to particular object, item of clothing, part of the body, etc.", https://en.oxforddictionaries.com/definition/fetish

I am a crossdresser, who is recently divorced, and I thought this was my opportunity to change my sex. I have been doing quite a lot of research and stumbled across your YouTube videos, as well as some others.

I now realize I have a gender fetish, but I would be unhappy to change my sex and then regret it. I haven't read your book, but what your (and those of others) videos say have touched my life. I now just hope and pray I can find a way to accept myself for who I am. For whatever reason, I have been put in this body with this fetish, and I need to learn to cope and not dwell on what could be.

I thank you again for helping me to not make a life altering change that is irreversible.

Brian

What's also interesting is that Brian thought his recent divorce gave him his opportunity to change his sex. A common theme I find with people who undergo sex change and later regret it is that an emotionally devastating event—such as divorce or a loved one's death—often propels them toward unnecessary surgery. I am so glad that Brian did some research first and realized he didn't need surgery to cope with a fetish. The next person wasn't so fortunate.

17 Cody's Botched Surgery "A mistake"

Many transgender people go to Thailand to save money on surgery. It's a fraction of the price of SRS in the U.S. and the surgical results are generally fine. Thailand also has the reputation of no waiting time and no screening, which appeals to people who want surgery right away and consider screening an unnecessary "roadblock."

> *I'm lost, broken and psychologically a wreck.*

The next email is from a person who went to Thailand for reassignment surgery and now lives with botched surgical results *and* blames himself for going through with what he calls "the ultimate plunge." (Warning: contains graphic surgical details.)

> *Hi Walt*
>
> *I recently had reassignment surgery done in Thailand. That was a mistake and it was a horrible operation. I'm now going back to living as a man again. When I say horrible I mean (sorry for the language) the doctor tucked my penis inside me and pulled it over my pubic bone and stitched the head of my penis to my skin for a clitoris. Now it feels like I have a constant erection and it has psychologically messed me up and I regret everything about this gender change.*

I should have never done this, and I blame myself but also, when I got evaluated by psychologists in Thailand they only sat down with me for no more than 30 minutes and they gave me the okay to proceed.

I'm lost, broken and psychologically a wreck. Can you give me any advice on what to do and where to go? I do want to thank you for your time reading this and I would love to help you in any way possible to keep this from happening to anyone else. I would love to help close these loopholes to keep people from doing exactly what I did.

Thank you again and I wish I read your story before I took the ultimate plunge.

Cody

I'm always amazed when critics will say Walt Heyer is the only one who ever regretted sex change, and he simply made a "mistake." But the letters and emails I receive—by the hundreds—tell a very different story: I am not alone. Sadly, I am joined by hundreds, if not thousands, of others who have been sold the hope of a false reality, and now seek a return to their true sex. The only "mistake," in my view, is in trusting gender specialists who, when GRS proves ineffective, blame the patient and pretend that his or her case is an exception.

18 Mother: Could Son's Boyhood Exposure to Pornography Be a Factor?

Exposure to pornography in childhood can cause unhealthy behaviors.

This email portrays how pornography and other disturbing childhood experiences can lead to gender and sexual confusion.

> *My ex-husband had multiple affairs and kept pornography where my son could see it.*

This information comes from Heather, the mother of Alex, a boy with gender issues. Heather describes the boy's home environment and asks if it could cause gender distress and dysphoria. The answer is an emphatic "Yes!"

My son, Alex, is 17 and the oldest of 7 siblings: 1 sister, 6 brothers. My ex-husband had multiple affairs and kept pornography where my son could see it. Several times I believe my ex took my son with him while he spent time at a woman's house. He did this so I wouldn't suspect he was cheating, but my son would always let something slip.

Anyways, when he was around 10 he touched his sister inappropriately. This was a one-time thing and we didn't discover until years later. When we did, he explained to us that he had some other unhealthy sexual thoughts. He engaged in a sexual relationship with an older man. He also said he hated his penis and wanted boobs. He wanted to be a girl, he says he felt this way for a long time.

Currently he is in a treatment facility for sex offenders, in August he will be 18 and free to leave. He has not committed any sexual crimes and is not a sex offender, but because of things he has said juvenile court felt this was where he needed to be sent.

As I said before, I only have 1 daughter. And girls tend to help more with chores, little babies, etc. My son says he always felt like I'd rather him be a girl, which is confusing to me. I don't think, or rather didn't realize that he was feeling that way. I wanted another girl, but 5 boys later it just wasn't in the cards for me.

I'm a huge tomboy. Football, baseball, no dresses etc. I feel so bad he felt this way.

He has told us that once he is released he plans to start hormone therapy and wants boobs as soon as possible. He says he identifies as bisexual because he thinks men are cute. He also says he wants to be hermaphrodite. But also says he wants a wife and children.

I am a Christian I believe God created us correctly and that society is getting out of control with all this transgender stuff. I love my son no matter what, but I think he's confused, and I don't know how to help him. I don't know how to encourage him or what to say?

Personally, I'd much rather him stay a boy and find a woman with big boobs to marry. My fear is that he is not prepared for how this will be affect the rest of us. I mean he wants his father to love him and his siblings are so important to him. Family is a big deal for him, but not everyone will be happy if he changes.

If there is anything you can do to advise either one of us, please do.

Thank you for your time

Heather

Alex's dad, apparently very unhealthy psychologically, enjoyed pornography and he did not hide his lust for pornography from his son. The pornography was available in the home where his son could entertain himself with the pictures. Heather made no attempt to make sure the pornography was locked up, burned up and or tossed in the trash, far away from young eyes. Heather knew about, but didn't protect Alex from, his father's frequent extramarital sexual encounters.

With all these abnormal, sexually explicit experiences at work in his young psyche, it is understandable that his view of men became skewed and he started to hate his penis and want female breasts. Perhaps he hated his penis because it represented his father and he didn't want to be like him. Alex wanted to be a girl, he says, for a long time.

This is one of many instances I have seen where gender dysphoria grows out of a child's efforts to protect themselves from wayward adults. Through psychotherapy Alex could begin the long road to recovery from his tormented childhood and avoid the wrong choice of changing genders.

19 Adam: Panicked and Suicidal Three Weeks Later

Gender advocates present the WPATH standards of care as the right (and only) way forward for gender dysphoric people. There are a host of issues with those standards, but the most relevant point here is that adhering to the standards will not prevent sex change regret.

> *I feel like I committed suicide, but I am still breathing...*

Adam, a male-to-female Canadian, followed the standards, yet just three weeks after surgery, he suffered panic attacks and suicide ideation. It is a telling point that he at first thought that transition was a "fantasy come true." But that begs the hard question that gender advocates cannot answer: how do you obtain truly informed consent to implement a fantasy through drugs and surgery?

Eleven months after his surgery, Adam reached out to me to share his raw emotions and disabling experiences that came after surgery. He says, "I feel I was egged on and left to hang myself."

> *I am 11 months after my sex change. I was on hormones for 3 years, lived as a female, I enjoyed it and felt like it was a fantasy come true.*

Then 3 weeks after my sex change I had bad panic attacks and felt suicidal. I had to take anti-anxiety medication and have been on sick leave from work ever since. I recently went to see a psychiatrist and was diagnosed with a form of depression worse than I had in the past, called dysthymic, meaning lower than regular moderate depression.

I now want to take legal action except nobody will take the blame as I signed an informed consent form, but I was not spoken to in person about the risks involved.

I also showed extreme ambivalence before surgery and did not want to go through with it, I am now having daily flashbacks and regretting my decision to go through with the surgery.

I feel if I had better insight I would not have had the surgery, but I did not know the chance for psychiatric morbidity was so high.

I feel I was egged on and left to hang myself, I feel like I committed suicide, but I am still breathing, wondering what your advice may be?

Regards

Adam (Ashley)

I replied:

Adam,

Your story sadly is all too common, and the sex change activists refuse to report the regret as if it never occurs. I will continue to write books, talk on radio and TV to expose this dark side of changing genders.

My two books Paper Genders and Sex Change, It's Suicide need to be in the hands of all who approve surgery, but they will not read the books. If they had, people like you, me and others would not have had the surgery.

It sounds like you have someone who is helping you deal with this but if you feel you need a bit more let me know.

Please understand you are not alone. I frequently get notes like this. Feel free to contact me and let me know how I can help.

Warm regards

Walt Heyer

I didn't hear back from him. After a couple of months, I reached out to him again.

Hello Adam,

It has been some time and I just wanted to check in and see how you are.

Warm regards

Walt

He replied right away. It's been 13 months since his surgery. He tried to get the attention of CPATH, the Canadian organization that oversees transgender health to report his regret and the need for more disclosure before putting people like him through surgery. But the response he receives is neither caring nor helpful.

Hi Walt

I am suffering on a daily basis and I feel resentment against the people who thought they were helping me.

I sent an email to Dr [name withheld] who is the head of the CPATH [Canadian Professional Association for Transgender Health] committee.

I told her my situation and she said she could not do anything about it except forward my query to the gender review board departmental head of staff.

The only action I could take is to file a lawsuit for lack of informed consent on behalf of the surgeon.

It's a lengthy and costly process but could be won, but there's no guarantee. Lack of "informed consent" is the legal and moral issue here.

Among other things that you mentioned the whole process is misleading and activist type psychologists and other people along the way seem to let you blunder your way in it.

Even if you think it is harmless it will come back to bite you, however apparently you and I are the exception and not the rule.

Adam

It's troubling that the head of the professional organization that sets the standards of care didn't want to know more about someone harmed by the process. But it certainly shows why the "standards of care" are suspect: even when confronted with evidence that sex change doesn't work, the complaint is shuffled to the side and the standards continue to guide people down the one-way road to gender affirmation.

Adam laments that he and I are the only ones, "the exceptions, not the rule." That's the narrative pushed by the gender change activists and the medical minions who profit from providing the surgery, but it's not true. The letters in this book show regretters exist and have been harmed in many ways by gender reassignment. It is a big reason why I write today: All the other Walts and Adams need to know that they are *not* alone, and that they *should* come forward for their own sake, and for the sake of others who might be similarly misled by the medical establishment.

I asked Adam if he would write something about his experience for this book. In his reply, he clearly articulates the same problems I see in the way the medical profession promotes surgery as the treatment for transgender people, without regard for those it harms. Adam poignantly verbalizes the consequences: "They promote this ideology thinking it's best for you, but they are not the ones dealing with the emotional suffering, constant pain and anguish."

Walt,

Yes, I can write 1/2 page, informative on the legal aspects anyhow.

Something like "People who consider going the extra step of living post op should still have the medical and psychological facts disclosed to them prior to SRS [Sex Reassignment Surgery]. There should be consequences for medical professionals who don't provide this".

As it stands there is only the WPATH [World Professional Association for Transgender Health] which is not legally enforceable; it only serves as an ethics guideline.

I can tell them what to expect from a pre-op perspective, but in regard to changing back from female to male again, there doesn't seem to be much support.

I mean the undertaking is huge and the resources are so limited I haven't heard much about the people who have regret and depression. What happens to them? Do they just go off and die?

Is that the idea of having SRS? I was under the impression that quality of life gets better after transition. Well, what percentage of the population is that for?

These mental health people here in Canada promote that stuff, but they fail to realize not everybody has the desired results.

Then when it backfires those same people want to bury their head in the sand. After it is too late, that's what really annoys me. They promote this ideology thinking it's best for you, but they are not the ones dealing with the emotional suffering, constant pain and anguish.

It is a lifelong commitment. I don't think people realize that it can be traumatizing for a long period of time afterwards. I was told it was one year for recovery. Maybe physically it was, but not mentally, it's more like 5 years.

Adam

Adam asks some excellent penetrating questions of the medical community about SRS results and calls out the mental health people who "bury their head in the sand" and "fail to realize not everybody has the desired results." But we know the organizations most involved in transgender health research—APA and WPATH—*do* realize not everyone has the desired results. Instead of studying it to find out why, they actively resist the evidence and apply pressure to suppress any such research. The third section of this book provides numerous examples of advocacy bias, suppression of research and intimidation of medical colleagues prevalent in the transgender health medical community today.

20 Noah: "What a Hoax"

Another common refrain in emails is the experience of an "aha moment" when the person acknowledges that no amount of surgery changes gender. The length of time varies from person to person, but when it comes, it is like having blinders taken off one's eyes.

Noah now knows an inconvenient truth: cosmetic surgery sold as a sex change is a hoax.

> *Here's my story... I just recently had the sex change operation a few months ago. My feelings of sex change regret started 3 weeks after surgery. I've already detransitioned back to living as a male. I realized that I am NOT female and cannot be.*
>
> *I feel better today thankfully than at any time in my life. Feelings of regret are powerful. Surgery reminded me that nothing can change me from the male I am. The operating table takes my genitals; that, for sure, will NOT make me a female. When I realized the surgery is all cosmetic surgery then I realized what a hoax it was to suggest or pretend I was a female.*
>
> *I'm not religious at all, but I'm sure others also have experienced the same realization and regret I have.*
>
> *Thank you for your time.*

Noah makes a remarkable point—he's male through and through and slicing off the obvious part does not change the DNA written into every cell in his body. Cosmetic surgery serves a sound ethical purpose when it improves what is there or replaces what is lost. But it fails miserably at creating a false reality. Therefore, it is so urgent that these voices be heard: how many others have awoken with this brutal clarity falling upon them, only to remain silent because they think no others have suffered the same?

21 Molly: "I need serious help ASAP"

Sometimes a person's regret is a consequence of the surgery itself, such as unexpected negative medical and physical consequences. For others, the surgical results are fine from a medical perspective, but one or more undiagnosed and untreated coexisting disorders leads to sex change regret.

Unfortunately, Molly, who was born Michael and lives in Europe, suffered both bad surgical results and a missed diagnosis of bipolar disorder. She now knows the proper treatment would have been to address the bipolar disorder and that gender surgery was never necessary. Personally, this was a tough story to confront: what begins as a rather clinical assessment of the past turns into an urgent "911" cry for help. How many more are out there, who have not yet called out as Molly (Michael) has?

> *Hello there Walt,*
>
> *I am a 37-year-old post-op transsexual woman from [country in Europe].*
>
> *I had my sex change in 2002 (14 years ago) although I have been living in the female role since 2000 (16 years ago). It never went well and I'm still on a waiting list for reconstructive cosmetic surgeries.*

Early on, I felt the sex change was successful. Now I feel my sex change was unsuccessful. It is still painful during intercourse after 14 years. It was really bad that the surgeon didn't even give me a proper clitoris and labia minora.

I came across your inspiring, helpful lifeline and wanted to get in touch. I don't know where to turn or to who, so I can detransition. To add to all the problems of unsuccessful sex change, I had a minor haemorraghic stroke in May 2015. I believe that was because of a perfect storm of cross hormonal therapy, estrogens and smoking and drinking.

I have a myriad of psychological issues and really believe I was rushed through the local Gender Identity Services Clinic in [major city] to get surgery completed, so much that the caregivers missed that I'm really a bipolar (depressive type) sufferer (survivor) and that I should've gotten life coach counseling and psychotherapy, instead of GRS [gender reassignment surgery] and hormones.

I want to detransition to be a male again. I need serious help ASAP, or I fear I may become a suicide statistic, or worse: severely depressed in a psychiatric hospital till I die or have a major haemorraghic stroke again!! And be rendered retarded and permanently disabled.

Please help. Let me know what you think. 👍 😊
I wish you all the happiness in the world and THANK YOU for your truthful website and life experiences.

Molly (Michael)

In reply, I thanked Molly for reaching out and assured her that hers is not the first case of someone getting pushed into surgical sex change instead of being evaluated for coexisting mental disorders. I strongly urged her to get help immediately for the depression.

In closing, I encouraged her:

> *Returning to Michael will be an emotional, psychological and medical support process that is not swift or easy.*
>
> *My heart is broken every time I get a letter as yours, but you should know I will do all I can to support you even when limited by the distance between us.*
>
> *Warm thoughts go out to you dear one; your sanity is returning as we exchange notes and bravo to you.*
>
> *Cheers and blessings and even silent prayer if you are inclined to do so.*
>
> *Walt*

Molly's regret didn't come early on; she was happy at first. Fourteen long years later, she's reached a point of desperation. She clearly sees that she should have had counseling and treatment of bipolar disorder.

Part 3—Facts and Information later in this book elaborates on the high prevalence of coexisting disorders in the transgender population and how important it is to diagnose and treat those before prescribing radical sex change procedures.

22 Corey Warns Others "to think very carefully"

After a person undergoes surgery and comes face-to-face with the reality that surgical sex change is simply cosmetic surgery and a person's sex doesn't change, regret may swiftly follow.

Gender-distressed people aren't emotionally or mentally equipped to grasp that truth. Worse, when they look for help, they're far more likely to find a gender-affirmation advocate rather than an ideologically neutral doctor who is going to look for real root cause of their distress. And with a bit of bad advice, their wishful thinking becomes a reality of pain or depression for themselves and their family and friends. As Corey so poignantly says below, such distressed people should "think very carefully about the consequences" for themselves and others.

> *When I opted for the sex change surgery I thought I was completely sure of what I was doing, I began to regret the decision a short time after the operation. Some might say I was experiencing post-op depression, but it was definitely more than that.*
>
> *I also suspect that many of the other patients at the hospital who had the same operation experienced similar feelings based on my discussions with them. If I were female, why wasn't*

I born with female genitalia? Sure, there are some intersexed people with ambiguous genitals, but I'm not at all intersexed. My chromosomes are the normal male XY, with absolutely no abnormalities. The reality is that I'm male, and no amount of surgery changes that fact. I'm now a post-op, and I've begun to transition (detransition) back to living as a male again. I feel it's the only way to be honest with myself and with society.

If you are considering this surgery, think very carefully about the consequences. Make sure that the doctor or counselor that's approving you people for the surgery looks for depression, fetishes, and other disorders first—there are too many unnecessary operations. No one talks about the pain or the emotional depression of regret not just for the trans-person but also all for the family and friends—they suffer also.

Corey

I appreciate that Corey acknowledges the deleterious effects on family and friends, who suffer devastation, too, but are often overlooked.

Thinking carefully about the choice of surgery is indeed wise, as the troubled veteran explains in the next story. He surely has troubles—but he is able to seek wise solutions for his burdens without adding on a lifetime of sex change regret.

23 Veteran Justin Avoids Surgery but Needs Hope

My inbox is endlessly full of dreadful stories about life's difficulties. This one is truly painful: a cash-strapped MTF veteran named Justin with an incredibly complex burden: he is diagnosed with highly-complex dissociative disorder[12] due to satanic ritual abuse, suicidal thoughts, ten years of cross-sex hormone use, and multiple doses of opiates every day for chronic pain. But the silver lining to his financial distress is: he has not yet fallen to the false hope a surgical sex change offers.

Justin rightly concludes that he needs to resolve the dissociative disorder before deciding on surgery. This veteran seems to have caught a tiny ray of hope from reading my story and seeing that I overcame issues like his. For that, I am grateful.

> *Hi, I read your book* A Transgender's Faith. *I read it in one sitting, all night last night. Then I started to read your other book* [Paper Genders] *but could not finish the chapter on lobotomies. That brings back memories of my satanic ritual abuse.*

---

[12] Previously known as multiple personalities.

I have been diagnosed with highly-complex DID/SRA [Dissociative Identity Disorder from Satanic Ritual Abuse], and gender dysphoria.

I have been on hormones for 10 years in order to stay alive. Otherwise I would have died. I have not had any gender-related surgeries. That has been highly recommended for me, but I am very poor and cannot afford them. I was suicidal until I started hormones, and the hormones enabled me to stay alive, now [provided] by prescription from the VA [Veterans Administration].

95% of my "inside people" identify as female, although the body was born male. My primary care doctor has the diagnosis for me as hermaphrodite, but I am not genetically intersexed [a medical condition where the genitalia or chromosomes are a combination of both male and female]. Since I was a small child I was thought of as "different" from everyone else.

I was put on social security disability, like you, because of the DID. My Christian counselor has told me that she thinks that gender surgery is a required part of my getting better from my DID.

I have come to the conclusion (which opinion my caregiver also shares) that my DID needs to be resolved prior to changing genders, and only then can things be seen more clearly if gender surgery is needed or not. Therefore, until the DID is resolved, no surgery. And then I am not sure if I will have the surgery.

Your biography reminds me of my own difficulties, with DID and also gender dysphoria. I believe your diagnosis of gender dysphoria was real, but a subset under your DID. And when your DID was resolved, then the gender problem was also resolved.

A complicating factor for me and my treatment: I am in constant pain due to a neck break that never properly healed. I am on very powerful opiates, several times every day. Also on muscle relaxant.

I noticed that you were able to get the help for your DID, which then resolved your gender dysphoria. That was life-saving for you!

There seems to be no hope for me at all.

Do you know of anywhere I might obtain help?

Thank you!!

Justin (aka Jessica)

I responded and gave him the best resources I could offer at the time. But he is not the last troubled veteran who will reach out to me, and I pray that you as a concerned reader might become part of a solution when others call for help.

24 Tim Escapes "Clutches of Sex Change Industry"

Like so many other gender specialists do, Tim's psychiatrist at the gender clinic rushed him toward cross-sex hormones, implants and surgeries, even though Tim expressed misgivings and wanted to explore the effect his childhood abuse had on his gender confusion. Tim's endocrinologist minimized his legitimate questions about long-term adverse effects of hormone replacement therapy.

When he was a child, Tim's parents abused him for their deviant purposes and the gender clinic offered to compound the abuse with permanent changes to his body. All so they can point to another "poster child" for sex reassignment.

Thankfully, Tim wisely said "No".

> Subject: *My Experience While in the Clutches of the Sex Change Industry*
>
> *I lived as a woman full time for six years and had cross-dressed regularly since I was a child. I was raised as a foster child by a gay male couple, one of whom presented full time as a woman. This 'woman' cross-dressed me and attacked my male gender identity. Both of them, who were cult leaders, physically, emotionally and sexually abused me, as well as prostituted me and used me to make child pornography. I wasn't their only victim.*

By the time I reached my twenties I was convinced that I was female and should live as such. I transitioned at 29, going through a gender clinic. I was one of their "poster child" patients as I was an IT professional working for a university. However, I was not happy and was starting to have my misgivings. They tried to rush me to get free breast implants as well as sex reassignment surgery with no effort to explore my misgivings. I had just become a Christian, so they assumed it was because of that and they had a gay Anglican priest talk to me to reassure me that God was ok with me changing sex.

After attending a talk on sexual abuse, I started relating my abuse memories, including the cross-gender conditioning I had undergone at the hands of my so-called foster mother to my gender confusion. It then occurred to me that I wasn't a true transsexual but was conditioned that way and that I was not so much running towards womanhood but running away from manhood.

I brought all that up to the psychiatrist, but she felt that was irrelevant to my Gender Dysphoria diagnosis. She was willing to have the unit psychologist work with me on my abuse issues and said that would help me feel more comfortable with going forward on my full sex reassignment. She pushed that I go ahead with the breast implants as that would make me feel better.

In parallel, I was also concerned with the possible long-term adverse effects of hormone replacement therapy, but those concerns were minimized by the endocrinologist even though my electrolytes were all off.

Looking around me I knew of one post-op suicide and several other very unhappy and remorseful post-ops. There were several post-ops who suffered severe physical complications, such as a fistula forming between the constructed vagina and rectum, bladder damage, and partial paralysis of the legs. Even in cases where the surgery had all the desired results, some post-ops suffered remorse and disappointment over the choice they had made. After the initial euphoria, it seemed like nothing was solved by going all the way.

I canceled the breast augmentation surgery and covertly weaned myself off the hormones. Eventually I stopped going to the gender clinic and did not return their calls. I felt I needed to give myself space to take the time to explore who I really was and to deal with my abuse issues. I was concerned about their continued pressure for me to continue down the sex reassignment road and their wanton disregard of the possibility that my gender discomfort was from other reasons. I had witnessed other patients pushed down this road to their detriment.

Eventually I detransitioned to my male identity. That was in 1991. I continue to be happy with the choice I've made.

Looking back, I see the gender clinic as more interested in their agenda and medical empire-building than in the well-being of myself or their other patients. I can only imagine it has become worse now that children are being encouraged to go down a path that they are not emotionally or intellectually mature enough to fully understand.

Tim

Tim's experience is a common theme I hear from people who regret. Gender clinics pressure patients to continue step-by-step down "the sex reassignment road" with wanton disregard for other issues that could be the cause of gender discomfort.

Thankfully, Tim had the wisdom and willpower to question, resist and walk away from the clinic and eventually, he resolved his gender conflict through counseling. He prevailed over "the clutches of the gender change industry" and avoided sex change surgery and its irreversible physical consequences.

25 Megan: "Being a man was a short escape from reality"

When the realization hits that an adopted transgender identity is simply a temporary escape, detransition is inevitable.

In a few words, this woman who took male hormones for nine months sketches the inside story of the trans man community, revealing the widespread psychological problems in others and her own misguided motivation to escape her "disastrous" life.

In my case, being a man was a short escape from reality, and I think that I'm not the first person to do this and regret it.

The specialists who urge the gender-distressed population toward transition fail to see what is obvious to this woman: the importance of treating the psychological problems first. Digging down into why people want a "second opportunity" or an "escape from reality" is vital and proper preliminary treatment that should precede the green light for cross-sex hormones and permanent surgical alterations.

Dear Walt,

After nine months of hormones (to go to man) I am going back to my original gender, the feminine. I have been looking at your website. It has a lot of information and I totally can identify with your thoughts.

I think that the change of sex is not the solution to anything, but the opposite.

Almost all the transsexuals that I have known have psychological problems and see the change of sex like a second opportunity, but it is not. In my case, being a man was a short escape from reality, and I think that I'm not the first person to do this and regret it.

Thank you for your work. By the way, I am member of Narcotics Anonymous (derived from Alcoholics Anonymous) and also believe in God as salvation. My life was so disastrous but not any longer.

An embrace.

Megan

Closing with "an embrace" seems most apropos—partly because Megan has embraced truth; a truth that is setting her free. Secondly because she realizes that recovery is not a solo affair: you need the love and support of others.

I am so heartened when people like Megan resonate with the information on my website, especially when they encounter it *before* sex change surgery and seeing it jolts them into reversing their sex change journey. The following story is another high-five to the power of the truth to set people free.

26 Amber, Age 20, Avoids Surgery

When I first decided to go public with my story more than a decade ago, I was aware it would generate controversy, but I decided it was worth it if I could help even one person avoid unnecessary sex change surgery.

That's why it means so much to receive an email like this one, where a 20-year-old natal male with gender distress reads the information on my website and decides surgery isn't needed. Difficult mental issues—bipolar disorder and post-traumatic stress disorder (PTSD)—must be dealt with first.

> *Hello, Walt!*
>
> *Before I discovered your site back in 2015, I was happy with my transgender identity. However, ever since I visited your site one day, I've had doubts ever since on a day by day basis. I never thought I would ever get the chance to undergo surgery because I feared I would never have enough money for it.*
>
> *As you mentioned, a majority of transgender individuals have untreated mental disorders. I have been diagnosed with bipolar and PTSD at the hands of my abusive father.*
>
> *There was a point in 2017 where I was okay with being a guy. My friend thinks I need to increase my dosages because now those feelings [of gender*

dysphoria] have resurfaced and I'm back to being the girl I feel inside. I'll admit, it hasn't been easy going back to this with the same arguments occurring at home like before.

Those same doubts and paranoia came back but I have finally realized something. Being transgender doesn't mean you NEED surgery. If I'm having these doubts now when I haven't even gone through HRT yet and I'm only 20, then I think it's best that I stay away from the operating table. I fear that I would want to go back the minute I wake up after surgery.

I never knew this before, but I have connected with other transgender girls who identify as "non-op transgender". They either realize that they may never have the finances for such treatment or they have the same thoughts and feelings that I do. They do what they can to deal with their identity.

So that's what I will be doing instead of keeping myself locked inside a constant cycle of doubt and fear that rages within, affecting me on the daily. When you keep mentioning how some post-op transsexuals commit suicide because they can never find inner peace and comfort, it only makes this worse and sometimes I felt like ending it before it even started.

So I can finally say, thanks to your studies and works, that I am a non-op transgender woman. I don't want the surgery. That doesn't mean that my mind won't change at some point when I decide to go through the therapy required before any sort of medical treatment. For the most part, it's what's best for me. Now, I'm still 20 years old, and I'm just now starting to experience life and its wonderful features. No one is forcing me to do anything.

So what I will be doing from here on out is not live in constant fear and experience the occasional mental breakdowns and live my life as Amber in privacy of my home and in the comfort and support of my family and friends.

So yes, thank you for making me seriously think about what it is that I truly am and not only saving me from possible mental trauma, but also the thousands of dollars that could possibly go to waste on a dream that may or may not be true.

Godspeed,

Amber :)

When some detractors deem me to be "transphobic" I think of this story, and how this young adult has become comfortable with a female identity while rejecting the false and dangerous hope of sex change surgery. That is exactly the "win" that each who comes to my website should gain: an understanding of the dangers of such surgery, and the will to resist its false hope.

27 Sean: Ten Years as Serena

I have heard from people who regretted their gender change from the moment they awake from the surgery. For others, it has taken 30 long years. And very often, I see regret emerging five to ten years after surgery.

This distressed individual shares his progression from childhood confusion and emotionally-disordered thinking to the ups and downs, euphoria, depression and anxiety of his transgender life, and now, to planning a transition back to male. He colorfully describes his "aha" revelation:

> *...once the euphoria was over and the pink clouds of happiness dispersed, I realized what I had done to myself.*

As his story shows, transgender identities are not innate and unchangeable.

> *Walt,*
> *In the past, I was convinced that I was supposed to be born a woman. I did have traumatic childhood, with violence, rape, grief, and instability. I had gender dysphoria from early childhood. I was dressing in girls' clothing and at age 11, I confessed to my friends that I was feeling a girl.*
> *I believed that transitioning was the answer to my problems. I had to transition. I consulted doctors and psychiatrists, started taking hormones, dressed*

up as woman and did facials and breast surgery and finally gender reassignment surgery. I lived as a man for 33 years and became a transwoman at the age of 33. I am now 43 and have been living as Serena, a woman, for 10 years.

In the initial stages of my womanhood, I was excited and happy. I had reached a lifetime goal and had become a woman. However, once the euphoria was over and the pink clouds of happiness dispersed, I realized what I had done to myself.

I realized that I had mutilated a healthy organ, that God had given me. I had a healthy and good-looking male body, I was handsome, and many women liked me, and some fell in love with me. I destroyed a body that God had created in perfect shape.

As Serena, I married a man and we divorced sometime later. I then had a relationship with another man and we split after few years. I had many male admirers. However, I lived a tense life. Always afraid that people would find out, I was born male. I was afraid of the consequences of this discovery. I lived in fear, and tried to live an introvert, recluse life, creating an air or mystery around me. This was not a life that suited me. I am a very outgoing and social person. I like to travel a lot and love people, animals and nature. I am a very passionate, loving and caring person. Living a socially isolated life, landed me in depression, stress and unhappiness.

I finally decided to break through the wall of fear, lies and deceit. I moved to [a place where no one knew me]. There I was confronted with myself and went through a heavy depressive episode. It took me half a year to come to accept me as a man again. This was unthinkable only 6 months ago.

Now I accept me as a man for the first time after 12 years. I am determined to gradually transition back to a man. The depression and tension have disappeared from my life. I am certain this is God's will and he helps and directs me towards returning to my original self. I am planning to share my story at some point when I am finished with detransitioning.

I agree with you. Majority of problems of TS people originate in early childhood and are routed in abuse, violence and neglect. I have, thank God, taken decision to live the way God created me. I am happy and proud I could take this decision. My family supports me, and I am on my way to become Sean. I will be in touch with you to share my detransitioning success in the coming period.

Cheers to you, dear Walt,

Sean

It's easy to see that Sean's troubles started with abuse, violence and neglect, not from some biological abnormality. This story is echoed in the next—it seems like pink clouds of happiness are spreading—yet when they disperse, they leave behind newfound clarity that one is created male or female.

28 Nineteen Years as Tiffany

Even bright people fall prey to transgender identity and its siren call of a utopian life.

This story illustrates the tragedy when emotional damage from childhood trauma is not addressed prior to transition: wasted years and ultimately, detransition.

Trent says he was delighted at living as a female at first, but these feelings of elation soon gave way to darker feelings. Now in his fifties, after nineteen years living as a woman, he wants to detransition.

> *I now realize all these years later, I believe*
> *I acted too swiftly.*

From the age of nine or ten, Trent felt trapped in the wrong body. He dated girls in high school but also had encounters with older men. In his twenties, Trent married, had children, and went on to serve ten years in the military. But the feelings of being a woman were still strong and he made the transition to Tiffany with cross-sex hormones, electrolysis on his facial hair, and breast implants, but no genital reconstruction.

Here are some of our email exchanges.

> *Walt,*
> *I was so glad to find your site and all the stories*
> *of people re-transitioning or detransition back to*

male. I now realize all these years later, I believe I acted too swiftly.

I transitioned to female originally. I never had the final surgery, but I did get breast augmentation.

I really wish I had not gotten implants; now I look forward to having the implants removed. I have started getting men's clothes, and such. It's really been so exciting going back to who I really am.

After 19 years living as a woman, I realized my desire to change genders came from deep-rooted childhood trauma, sexual trauma, environment and family relationships.

Like you said, in one of your writings. I totally relate to this:

> *"Hidden deep underneath the make-up and female clothing was the little boy carrying the hurts from traumatic childhood events, and he was making himself known. Being a female turned out to be only a cover-up, not healing."*

Having a someone like you, a role model who has detransitioned, is helpful to me. I really appreciate you allowing me to share my story with you. I look forward to hearing from you, at your convenience.

Trent

Walt Heyer <waltsbook@yahoo.com> wrote:

Trent,

Thanks for your note. It is more common that most realize that detransition is desired and occurs. Thankfully you did not go through the last step of transitioning as the return is much easier.

Most often the move to change gender happens too easily and too quickly and is part of the reason why over 40% of transgenders will attempt suicide.

Not having bottom surgery is characteristic of "transvestites" as they often have some surgeries, but not bottom surgery.

Thanks again and all the best.

Cheers,

Walt Heyer

Several things in Trent's story reinforce common themes we're seeing in the emails: acknowledging his regret took nineteen long years and the desire to change genders originated in childhood and sexual trauma. I would add one more thing we can learn: it's never too late to be free from the trans life and live authentically.

29 Eric: "My doctor lied"

Regretters are scorned, ridiculed and dismissed by trans activists as not being "real" even though gender specialists said they were. As this person says, "I'm finding the community backlash to be difficult."

Eric also found out the hard way that virtually no medical support exists for someone who wants to detransition, creating a major roadblock to this process. Medical support for people with gender dysphoria is all directed toward transition and after transition, all help disappears.

But the overwhelming tragedy for Eric is the egregious medical malfeasance he suffered at the hands of his primary care physician when he originally went for care for his gender dysphoria. Unknown to Eric, the physician had an ulterior motive (which he admitted when confronted) to enable greater access to sex reassignment surgery. Without disclosing his personal interest, this doctor wrongly approved Eric's life-altering surgery. But knowing that now won't bring Eric's original body back. The patient is obviously the one to suffer the consequences of impaired health and diminished well-being.

> *Dear Walt,*
>
> *I'm trying to come out as a regretter, and I'm finding the community backlash to be difficult and the lack of medical support to be troubling.*

I discovered that my primary care doctor had lied to me about my course of care. He told me we were following the WPATH [The World Professional Association for Transgender Health] Standards of Care. He told me I didn't need a psychologist. He told me to get surgery to cut my dependence on hormones. He told the surgeon in writing that I'd met all the standards of care and was approved for surgery. He told me the function would be good.

All of it: not true.

My feeling and function have been diminished. The doctor who approved me lied to the surgeon about my qualifications. He admitted verbally when I confronted him he was trying to enable greater access to surgery. I'm now told I can never stop hormones without risking my length and quality of life.

I want my original natural body and health back. I want to do something for my family and do all I can to help prevent this from happening to others. It's horrible.

Thank you

Eric

Horrible, indeed—but so important that this valiant man bring his story forward. When he does—as a brave few have done already—we will see good results, as reported in the next account by a man who fortunately dealt with his primary psychological issues and avoided surgery.

30 Wyatt Avoids Surgery

Every once in a long while, in among the emails that tell of sex change regret and heartache, I receive an email from someone who avoids surgery. For Wyatt, a man with gender dysphoria, a psychiatric hospital appropriately tested him for psychiatric disorders and saved him from the heartbreak of unnecessary sex change surgery.

Now he has strong opinions about surgeons who perform surgery on people without testing them first for psychiatric disorders: In his view, they are "quacks" and "charlatans."

> *Mr. Heyer, I am glad you talk about regrets.*
>
> *You have no idea how psychiatric disorders effecting transsexualism [are actually] a type of depression disorder. I was in the psychiatric hospital because I thought I was girl. I failed the dexamethasone suppression test which showed that I had major clinical depression. I also had thyroid tests for depression, ECG brain wave scan and lots of psyche tests. They told me that surgeons would not operate on me without medical and psychiatric clearance, so I avoided surgery.*
>
> *The problem is that surgery does not treat major depression and neither do hormones. They gave me desipramine [an antidepressant]. I was going to go to Dr Stanley Biber who did over 5,000 SRS now his*

successor, Dr. Marci Bowers did 1,100 under 10 years.

They are quacks.

As far as I know they do not require either chemical test for major depression or talk therapy for reactive adjustment disorder of childhood and your data show half of patients have an adjustment disorder.

I know lots of people who regret SRS. I tell you—hormones and surgeries are not acceptable treatments for clinical depression or adjustment disorders.

How can these quacks parade on SRS forums?

Why does the research on psych disorders that mask as gender dysphoria come from other countries other than US? I talked to Biber and Bowers, and they are charlatans. They do not have training in psychiatry.

Wyatt

Wyatt is correct: sex change surgery and cross-gender hormones are not appropriate treatment for major clinical depression. Thankfully, in his case, mental health screening provided an accurate diagnosis and saved him from falling prey to sex change regret.

31 Thank You Emails

With so much sadness rolling into sexchangeregret.com, it's a blessing when "thank you" emails pop up. I appreciate the encouragement from those who are in the trenches of the struggle, and I share these with you as a way of thanking you for joining in fighting for these many distressed souls.

Subject: Thank you

Sir, what a brave and, therefore, generous man you are. Just recently, I became acquainted with you and your work. (You write very well, which I admire, because clear, rational, and compassionate communication is a gift and because you effectively articulate your desire to serve those who are suffering greatly and who need wise counsel, which, to be wise, must be wrapped in genuine love.)

Sir, I hope, as you close your eyes each evening and reflect on your day, you realise that someone, who will never be able to repay you, might be spared a continuation of suffering because you spoke on his/her behalf: a true mitzvah. You and your work are on my prayer list--though I did not know I was praying for you. I smile as I write this. Thank you, Sir.

Carly, A still grieving sister

Thank you from Spain

This is the first day of my second adolescence. A chance to live without fear and free.

Cheers, my friend. For all this (sic) people in our same situation you are one angel who experimented and suffered to discover the truth and show us the way.

Now we have the benefit of this new life.

Thanks, Walt.

Javier

32 Trans Activist Says It's "Bullshit"

The letters in this book tell a gripping story of mental anguish, false hope, untreated psychological disorders and wasted years lost in pursuit of a sex change.

The loud voices for political correctness continue to spread the false idea that the strong desire to change genders is innate and unchangeable. Based on that lie, they lobby lawmakers to outlaw access to all psychotherapy. Chief among these are the APA and WPATH (see the appendix for evidence).

A transgender person does not need to experience a spiritual epiphany to realize at some point that changing genders is madness and to make the sane choice of detransitioning. These stories demonstrate that the knowledge can come gradually or quickly from first-hand experience. Bravo to the people who courageously examine their lives and take steps to restore some of the sanity that has been lost.

I will close this section of first-hand accounts with comments from a transgender activist who originally adopted a female persona as a teenager and decades later detransitioned back to male.

Alexis Arquette (formerly Robert Arquette), a transgender performer and activist, returned to living as a man before his death on September 11, 2016, at the age of 47. Arquette had small but memorable roles in the movies

Pulp Fiction and *The Wedding Singer* and was a force for transgender rights.

Arquette's transition to woman was featured in the 2007 documentary, "Alexis Arquette: She's my Brother." But there was no film about Alexis detransitioning back to Robert in 2013.

In the many media tributes after his death, few mention his decision to stop living as a woman. However, one piece in *The Hollywood Reporter* does speak of Arquette's gender struggles through an interview with close friend and fellow drag performer, Sham Ibrahim.

Clearly, even well-known and talented transgender individuals who are embraced and accepted in their chosen gender can continue to vacillate and may decide to return to their birth sex.

> In 2013, amid increasing health complications, Alexis ... began presenting herself as a man again, telling [her close friend] Ibrahim that "'gender is bullshit.' That 'putting on a dress doesn't biologically change anything. Nor does a sex-change.' She said that 'sex-reassignment is physically impossible. All you can do is adopt these superficial characteristics but the biology will never change.'" That realization, Ibrahim suspects, was the likely source of her deep wells of emotional torment.[13]

It's certain that many have "deep wells of torment" like Arquette. Every day, more people come forward to share their detransition stories on YouTube. Look in the

---

[13] Abramovich, S., "A Tear in the Ocean": The Final Days of Alexis Arquette, *The Hollywood Reporter*, September 13, 2016, accessed on August 17, 2018 at http://www.hollywoodreporter.com/news/final-days-alexis-arquette-a-928507

appendix for other sources of first-hand accounts of detransition.

For me, it was my faith in the power and grace of Jesus Christ that brought my redemption and restoration after a lifetime of gender confusion, a sex change, and living eight years as a woman. I needed effective, intense psychotherapy to resolve the psychological issues that drove my desire to change genders.

It is high time to stop using the blunt instrument of gender reassignment to treat a condition that clearly requires a more complex and nuanced approach. Instead, we need to encourage effective medical and psychological treatment *for all* who suffer any degree or form of gender distress.

PART 2

Children

It is hard to hear these many stories from adults who regret their choices. It is harder still when choices are being made for children, or adolescents are being swayed into making foolish choices. And these are the most urgent stories: children and adolescents should look to adults for sound counsel, and not be misled into consenting to treatments that eliminate a future that they cannot yet fully comprehend. How can a child or young teen truly consent to arrested sexual development, potential chemical or surgical sterilization, writing off the prospect of marriage and intimacy as enjoyed by their sex, of pursuing "pink clouds of happiness" when they don't know a thunderhead from a wisp of cumulus? Following are the truly troubling stories of youth misdirected to a false future.

33 Teenage Max: "I wish I had listened to you"

Doctors have no scientific basis for their recommendation to prescribe hormone blockers, cross-sex hormones or transition surgeries for children with gender dysphoria. The truth is that no one can predict whether a gender dysphoric child will feel the same way years later.

Kristina Olson, a child transgender research psychologist at the University of Washington, puts it this way: "We just don't have definitive data one way or another." That's why Olson is leading a study of 300 trans children that will track outcomes over 20 years, "to be able to, hopefully, answer which children should or should not transition," she said.[14]

In other words, doctors simply don't know right now. Someday, perhaps, but in the meantime the damage to this generation of trans kids is underway. Parents are at a loss, and early adopters of teenage transition are contacting me with regret.

---

[14] Shaban, B., Campos, R., Villarreal, M., Horn, M. and Carroll, J., "Transgender Kids Could Get Hormone Therapy at Earlier Ages" , The Investigative Unit of NBC Bay Area, May 18, 2017, accessed on July 10, 2017 at https://www.nbcbayarea.com/investigations/Transgender-Kids-Eligible-for-Earlier-Medical-Intervention-Under-New-Guidelines-423082734.html

Recently an email arrived in my inbox with the subject "I wish I had listened to you" that shows the human casualties from the "grand experiment" on children. Max, now in his mid-twenties, transitioned in his teens and now realizes he was too young to make the decision to take cross-sex hormones and undergo surgery.

Max's young body is permanently damaged because doctors have no definitive idea as to who will persist in a condition of gender dysphoria and yet propose irreversible treatments for young people who feel conflicted about gender. As Max found out, even strongly held feelings change.

> *Subject: I wish I had listened to you*
>
> *I'm only in my mid [twenties]. I transitioned in my teens and had surgery. I was [too] young to make such a decision.*
>
> *I've sunken into such a deep regret. I don't even feel transgender anymore. I feel like my old self. I am happy with a female appearance but that is all I really needed.*
>
> *I feel like I was brainwashed by the transgender agenda and by gender norm expectations. I would do anything to [have] my penis back.*
>
> *My feelings were confusing, and I thought they would never go away. I'm just a guy who's really in touch with my feminine side.*
>
> *I can't believe what I've done to my life. And now I have no choice but to take hormones forever. I don't know what to do. I feel like I'm losing my mind. All I would have had to do was discontinue my hormones and everything would have been alright. I honestly feel 100% normal and okay . . . if only I had never had that surgery.*
>
> *Max*

This story merits further thought: this young man's doctors would no doubt say that Max gave fully informed consent to have his perfectly healthy male anatomy sliced away. But how can that be so, when you see him awakening to what he has lost, and recognizing the surgery as a mistake? How could a teenager truly understand what he was giving up by eliminating his normal sexual development; the opportunity to become a husband and father; the blessing of living with the normal body chemistry of a man rather than force-feeding his system female hormones—for life—and with that a host of life-long medical risks? Fortunately, some are receiving better counsel—such as the daughter in the next story.

34 Brie Jentry and her teenage daughter

Brie Jentry is the mother of a teen desister, Maxine (a pseudonym), and supported her daughter in what turned out to be a loving and effective way. Together they embarked on an extensive exploration of what Maxine was feeling, but Mom set some boundaries to avoid harm. Jentry says:

> Gender dysphoria is real, and it causes real suffering. My daughter was in deep, profound, pain...
>
> I didn't agree to let her subject herself to significant bodily harm in an attempt to treat her dysphoria. From the very first announcement, I let her know that she could cut her hair however she wanted, wear whatever clothing she wanted, and use whatever name she chose.
>
> I supported her in her discomfort, to the best of my ability, and I also let her know that discomfort and confusion are legitimate aspects of a meaningful, deeply explored life.[15]

Brie Jentry is now spokesperson for 4thWaveNow, which according to their website is "a community of parents & others concerned about the medicalization of gender-atypical youth and rapid-onset gender dysphoria

---

[15] https://4thwavenow.com/2017/10/25/born-in-the-right-body-introducing-4thwavenows-new-spokesperson-mom-of-a-teen-desister/

(ROGD)." The website offers a voice of sanity and balanced information for parents of trans kids.

Maxine has described her early teen journey towards a transgender identity and back to female beautifully and transparently in an interview posted on 4thWaveNow.com.[16] After time in psychotherapy, she came to some self-understanding about her dysphoria:

> Discomfort about your body and sometimes dysphoria are a normal part of being a teenager and having your body change...
>
> I used being trans to try and escape being scared about being small and weak. I thought that if I presented myself as a man I'd be safer.

Desistence versus persistence

Research studies show that when children with GD are *not* encouraged toward social transition, *and* psychotherapy is made available for the child and the family, the results are astounding. **Eighty to ninety-five (80-95%) percent accept their biological sex by late adolescence.**[17,18] In other words, the children outgrow or resolve their gender dysphoria; they "desist" from pursuing transition.

---

[16] "It's not conversion therapy to learn to love your body: A teen desister tells her story", November 7, 2017, accessed on October 4, 2018, at https://4thwavenow.com/2017/11/07/a-teen-desister-tells-her-story/

[17] Cohen-Kettenis PT, Delemarre-van de Waal HA, Gooren LJ. The treatment of adolescent transsexuals: changing insights. J Sexual Med 2008;5:1892–1897.

[18] Cantor, J., "Statistics faulty on how many trans-kids grow up to stay trans-?," *Sexology Today!*, December 17, 2017, accessed on August 6, 2018, at http://www.sexologytoday.org/2017/12/faulty-statistics-on-how-many-trans.html

As mother Brie Jentry puts it, "desisters" are those who once thought of themselves as trans but do not currently see themselves that way. Jentry clearly articulates the role of the parent of a trans child:

> After initial hesitation, I knew my child was not "born into the wrong body" and that as her parent, I would be doing more long-term good (and also less long-term harm) by offering her the time and tools she needed to see herself as whole, capable, and "authentic" as she was instead of affirming that there was something wrong with her.
>
> Puberty suppressants, cross-sex hormones, and surgery, all have life-long consequences. Shouldn't the focus be on helping people learn to accept themselves, in all their messy, unmatched, contradicting, and possibly limiting, glory?

By applying these principles over two years with her daughter, Brie Jentry gave her daughter the greatest gift: space and time to discover who she is and to accept and love herself just as she is.

35 What we know about trans-kids

Child gender specialists admit there is *no data* and *no test* that can truly determine that a distressed child is, or is not, transgender. As Kristina Olsen said, "We just don't have definitive data..."[19]

On the other hand, as we'll see next, strong *evidence does exist* to show that most gender distressed children, if not transitioned and affirmed during childhood, will grow up to accept their natal sex. It is also clear that when adults affirm children in the opposite gender and doctors provide hormone blockers to delay puberty, the natural healing process is disrupted, and children get locked into a transgender life.

Yet gender advocates herd—if not outright drive—parents and children to a one-way journey of social, hormonal and physical transition. And they do it without even one controlled, randomized study saying that such treatments are safe or effective in the long term. It's a grand experiment on children, with many risks and consequences. Adults who give children the right to select

---

[19] Shaban, B., Campos, R., Villarreal, M., Horn, M. and Carroll, J., "Transgender Kids Could Get Hormone Therapy at Earlier Ages", op. cit.

a gender have total disregard for the long-term consequences of regret, unhappiness and suicide.

a) Reasons for identifying as trans

Some young people desire to identify as the opposite sex to escape the pain of a traumatic event or a perceived abandonment or loss. They subconsciously want to dissociate from who they are and become someone else. Gender change promises a fresh start, free from the past. The perceived abandonment can be a simple childish misconception, as Nathan shared in his email, when he felt replaced in his parents' affection by the birth of his baby sister.

Some research indicates that autism is a risk factor for gender dysphoria. One study found the incidence of autism among the gender dysphoric children was 7.8 percent, 10 times higher than the rate in the general population.[20] Another group reported that more than half of 166 young people referred to a major gender clinic had features of autism. Of that number, nearly half of those who scored in the severe range had not previously been assessed for autism.[21] Researchers don't yet know why the two conditions appear to be linked.

Other teens or pre-teens today want to identify as the other gender because, like Max and Maxine, they don't feel they fit into stereotypical male or female roles or they are

---

[20] de Vries AL, Noens IL, Cohen-Kettenis PT, van Berckelaer-Onnes IA, Doreleijers TA, Autism spectrum disorders in gender dysphoric children and adolescents, J Autism Dev Disord. 2010 Aug;40(8):930-6. doi: 10.1007/s10803-010-0935-9.

[21] Skagerberg E, Di Ceglie D, Carmichael P, Brief Report: Autistic Features in Children and Adolescents with Gender Dysphoria., J Autism Dev Disord. 2015 Aug;45(8):2628-32. doi: 10.1007/s10803-015-2413-x..

having difficulty with the changes in adolescence or they want to fit in with their friends. We're hearing more and more about teens identifying as transgender simply after spending time on social media.

Dr. Richard B. Corradi, psychiatrist and Professor Emeritus at Case Western University Psychiatry Department, gives a plausible explanation for adolescent gender dysphoria based on his years in psychiatry. He says gender confusion can be a mechanism for coping with the overwhelming changes happening in adolescence:

> Gender confusion—the wish to be the opposite sex, or even to be no sex at all (non-gendered)—can simply be a young person's temporary pause in resolving the conflict between the safety of secure parental attachments and the compelling but frightening urges of adult sexuality and autonomy. The vast majority of such defense mechanisms are transient, useful when the storms of adolescence are most intense, but no longer necessary as a more stable sense of self emerges.[22]

A recent phenomenon among adolescents and young adults is rapid-onset gender dysphoria (ROGD), the sudden outbreak of gender dysphoria among friends, primarily females who did not exhibit the symptoms of gender dysphoria previously. Lisa Littman, behavioral and social sciences professor at Brown University, is studying ROGD to "better understand this phenomenon, its implications and scope" and "to generate hypotheses,

---

[22] Corradi, RB, "Psychiatry Professor: 'Transgenderism' Is Mass Hysteria Similar To 1980s-Era Junk Science", *The Federalist*, November 17, 2016, accessed on August 15, 2018 at
http://thefederalist.com/2016/11/17/psychiatry-professor-transgenderism-mass-hysteria-similar-1980s-era-junk-science/

including the role of social and peer contagion in the development of this condition."[23]

I say "Bravo" to Professor Littman, Dr. Corradi and others like them who don't blindly promote puberty blockers and transition for adolescents but rather look for causes and effects, which will lead to the development of non-invasive treatment protocols based on actual science.

The variety of reasons why adolescents identify as transgender illustrates the vital necessity for parents and counselors to take time with the teen to uncover what is driving the desire to change gender, *before* pursuing any steps toward transition.

b) Social transition is not harmless

Dr. Kenneth Zucker, who worked with hundreds of children with gender issues over many years in Toronto, says that social transition of young people (adopting cross-gender clothes, hair style, pronouns, name) is itself a "psychosocial treatment" that will influence the outcomes. He says that children who socially transition will be more likely to persist in the opposite gender than those who do not socially transition. He makes the following prediction and argument in his 2018 article:

> Thus, I would hypothesize that when more follow-up data of children who socially transition prior to puberty become available, the persistence rate will be extremely high. This is not a value judgment – it is simply an empirical prediction. Just like Temple Newhook et al. (2018) argue that some of the

---

[23] Littman L (2018) Rapid-onset gender dysphoria in adolescents and young adults: A study of parental reports. PLoS ONE 13(8): e0202330. https://doi.org/10.1371/journal.pone.0202330

children in the four follow-up studies included those who may have received treatment "to lower the odds" of persistence, **I would argue that parents who support, implement, or encourage a gender social transition (and clinicians who recommend one) are implementing a psychosocial treatment that will increase the odds of long-term persistence.**[24]

c) Puberty blockers are not harmless

Puberty blocking medications are recommended by gender medical professionals to give pre-puberty gender dysphoric children "more time" before the onset of puberty to decide whether to proceed with gender transition. In the United States, the FDA has not approved the drugs for treatment of gender dysphoria. In other words, they are being used "off-label." Off-label status reflects that the use has not been proven in clinical trials to be safe and effective.[25]

The blockers stop the development of some secondary sex characteristics that occur naturally during puberty. In girls, breasts develop, body fat creates a softer, rounder appearance, and menstruation commences. In boys, the musculature of the body changes and grows stronger, the testicles develop, facial hair grows, and the voice deepens.

[24] Zucker, K. J. (2018). The myth of persistence: Response to "A Critical Commentary on Follow-Up Studies and "Desistance" Theories about Transgender and Gender Non-Conforming Children" by Temple Newhook et al. (2018). International Journal of Transgenderism. https://doi.org/10.1080/15532739.2018.1468293

[25] Hruz, PW, Mayer, LS, McHugh, PR, Growing Pains / Problems with Puberty Suppression in Treating Gender Dysphoria, The New Atlantis, Spring 2017, https://www.thenewatlantis.com/docLib/20170619_TNA52 HruzMayerMcHugh.pdf

Additionally, these medications have harmful effects that should alarm parents. They arrest bone growth and decrease bone mass which can lead to increased risk of bone fractures as young adults and reduced adult height. The drugs prevent the sex-steroid dependent organization and maturation of the adolescent brain and inhibit fertility.[26]

John Whitehall, professor of Paediatrics at Western Sydney University, writes about the medical consequences of using puberty suppression drugs on the brain. Studies in sheep show lasting damage to the area of the brain that integrates cognition, memory and emotions. That part of the brain was enlarged and the function of many of its genes altered. The affected sheep demonstrated sustained reduction in memory and an increase in emotional lability, a term which means exaggerated changes in mood or affect in quick succession.[27]

Scientists in the United States report similar negative effects on the brains of adults who took these drugs. Journal studies published in 2006 and 2007 showed brain abnormalities in the area of memory and executive functioning among adult women who received blockers for

---

[26] Gender Dysphoria in Children, American College of Pediatricians Position Statement, June 2017, accessed on August 5, 2018 at https://www.acpeds.org/the-college-speaks/position-statements/gender-dysphoria-in-children

[27] Whitehall, J, Experimenting on Gender Dysphoric Kids, Quadrant Online, July 24, 2018, accessed on September 19, 2018, https://quadrant.org.au/magazine/2018/07/experimenting-children-gender-dysphoria/

gynecologic reasons.[28,29] No studies on children are available.

Prescribing medication that has not been studied for use on biologically normal gender dysphoric youth and is known to interfere with brain development and fertility— why would anyone do this to children?

d) Puberty blockers create trans adults

Giving trans children puberty blocking drugs, the experimental approach, starting as early as ten years of age, is now common practice in gender clinics across the U.S. Just as Zucker predicted, the persistence rate (progressing toward full transition) under this approach is extremely high.

The gender specialists who advocate for pre-puberty affirming and transition protocols are *causing* the gender dysphoric children to lock into a transgender identity. They are manufacturing transgender people out of suffering children who would likely grow out of the desire to change genders if not affirmed. I call this child abuse.

This is demonstrated dramatically in the results of a follow-up study of 70 pre-puberty children given puberty blockers. It showed that *all* the children who were affirmed

---

[28] Grigorova M, Sherwin B, Tulandi T (2006), Effects of treatment with leuprolide acetate depot on working memory and executive functions in young premenopausal women, Psychoneuroendocrinology. 31. 935-47. 10.1016/j.psyneuen.2006.05.004.

[29] Craig M, Fletcher PC, et.al. (2007), Gonadotropin hormone releasing hormone agonists alter prefrontal function during verbal encoding in young women, Psychoneuroendocrinology. 32. 1116-27. 10.1016/j.psyneuen.2007.09.009.

and given puberty blockers eventually embraced a transgender identity and requested cross-sex hormones.[30]

The American College of Pediatricians (ACP) has this to say about the follow-up study's results:

> Normally, 80 percent to 95 percent of pre-pubertal youth with GD do not persist in their GD. To have 100 percent of pre-pubertal children choose cross-sex hormones suggests that *the protocol itself* [emphasis added] inevitably leads the individual to identify as transgender.
>
> There is an obvious self-fulfilling nature to encouraging a young child with GD to socially impersonate the opposite sex and then institute pubertal suppression.[31]

Youngsters who continue past the stage of puberty suppression to taking cross-sex hormones and having genital surgery will be rendered permanently infertile, unable to have genetic offspring in the future, to their everlasting regret.

e) Affirmation tells a child, "Something is wrong with who you are"

I believe another effect of adults playing "gender make believe" with children is the destruction of the child's core identity. Telling a girl that she's a boy, or a boy he's a girl,

---

[30] De Vries ALC, Steensma TD, Doreleijers TAH, Cohen-Kettenis, PT. Puberty suppression in adolescents with gender identity disorder: a prospective follow-up study. J Sex Med 2011;8:2276-2283.

[31] Gender Dysphoria in Children, American College of Pediatricians Position Statement, June 2017, op. cit.

plants the destructive notion deep inside their young psyches that the essence of who they are is wrong.

Affirming a child as the opposite gender reinforces the deep discomfort already undermining his or her identity. Children internalize the idea that the natal girl or boy is not someone to be loved or embraced, but eradicated.

Overwhelmed by the weight of these messages cloaked as "affirmation" and a lack of attention to the real issues driving the desire to switch gender appearances, too many attempt suicide.

f) Suicidal behavior

An early informal survey of transgender individuals found a suicide-attempt rate among transgender adolescents of 45%.[32] More recently, a peer-reviewed study[33] analyzed suicide attempts among young transgender-identified Americans between the ages of 11 and 19. The rate of suicide behavior for all teenagers is 14%. For transgender teens, the attempted suicide rates are double or tripled that, depending on gender:

- For female-to-male adolescents: One in every two (50%) attempt suicide.

- For gender non-conforming adolescents (neither exclusively male or female): Four out of ten (40%) attempt suicide.

---

[32]Grant JM Ph.D., et.al, "Injustice at Every Turn: A Report of the National Transgender Discrimination Survey", op. cit., p.82

[33] Toomey RB, Syvertsen AK, Shramko M, Transgender Adolescent Suicide Behavior, Pediatrics, Oct 2018, e20174218, accessed on September 18, 2018, http://pediatrics.aappublications.org/content/early/2018/09/07/peds.2017-4218

- For male-to-female adolescents: Three out of
  ten (30%) attempt suicide.

Medical doctors who specialize in pushing children to transition tell parents that their gender dysphoric children *must* proceed with transition to keep them from killing themselves, but there's no proof. Advocates are quick to blame the suicide behavior on lack of acceptance by society and family, or a delay to transition, but Drs. Bailey and Blanchard who research this say the opposite:

> There is already plenty of reason, however, to doubt the conventional wisdom that all the trouble is caused by delaying gender transition of gender dysphoric persons. We have already mentioned the fact that transitioned adults who had been gender dysphoric (i.e., "transsexuals") have increased rates of completed suicide. Their transition did not prevent this, evidently. Suicide (and threats to commit suicide) can be socially contagious. Thus, social contagion may play an important role in both suicidality and gender dysphoria itself. Autism is a risk factor for both gender dysphoria and suicidality.[34]

The next email is a harbinger and warning of the regret teens choosing gender change today will experience a decade or so from now. It dramatically confirms that gender specialists who tell young adults that their gender dysphoric feelings will never change and then urge them to transition needlessly burden innocent, hurting people with lifelong harm. The truth is: feelings can, and do, change.

---

[34] Bailey PhD JM, Blanchard PhD R, Suicide or transition: The only options for gender dysphoric kids?, accessed September 19, 2018, https://4thwavenow.com/2017/09/08/suicide-or-transition-the-only-options-for-gender-dysphoric-kids/

36 Teenage transitioner, Derrick, says, "I don't have those feelings anymore"

The tragedy of treating transient feelings with permanent solutions is counted in real people's lives. No matter how strongly conflicted the child or teenager feels, he or she is still too immature to count the consequences of transition.

This thirty-something man, Derrick, transitioned to female in his late teens. Now in his early thirties, he laments the change because he doesn't feel like a woman anymore. Like so many others, his feelings of being a woman went away after he sought counseling for childhood issues.

We learn from this man what I learned in my own life: the transgender feelings are not permanent, immutable, or deep-seated in the brain. Feelings, no matter how powerful, do not justify taking hormones and undergoing surgery.

I transitioned to female beginning in my late teens and changed my name in my early 20s, over ten years ago. But it wasn't right for me; I feel only discontent now in the female role. I was told that my transgender feelings were permanent, immutable, physically deep-seated in my brain and could

NEVER change, and that the only way I would ever find peace was to become female. The problem is, I don't have those feelings anymore. When I began seeing a psychologist a few years ago to help overcome some childhood trauma issues, my depression and anxiety began to wane but so did my transgender feelings. So, two years ago I began contemplating going back to my birth gender, and it feels right to do so. I have no doubts--I want to be male!

I did have orchiectomy [the removal of one or both testicles], and that happened before my male puberty had completed, so I have a bit of facial hair which I never bothered to get electrolysis or laser for, and so the one blessing about all this is that with male hormone treatment I can still resume my male puberty where it was interrupted and grow a full beard and deep voice like I would have had if transgender feelings hadn't intruded upon my childhood. My breasts are difficult to hide though, so I'll need surgery to get rid of them. And saddest of all, I can never have children, which I pray God will give me the strength to withstand that sadness.

Derrick

Transition has consequences which teenagers aren't mature enough to understand fully: how can a boy who is in many ways still a child "consent" to surgically eliminate fatherhood from his future?

Sadly, Derrick lost ten years of his life and he pays the penalties for his misdirection. He will require male hormone (testosterone) treatment for life because, without testicles, his body won't produce it naturally. Artificially administered hormones carry the ongoing risk of adverse side effects. His chest is permanently scarred. And his saddest realization is that the transition procedures rendered him sterile and unable to have children.

How many more teenage boys and girls with gender confusion will see their transgender feelings wane in their twenties and pray to "withstand that sadness" like Derrick did, before sex change for children is discredited?

PART 3

FACTS *and*

INFORMATION

37 Detransitioning

Detransitioning is the process of reversing the effects of the original sex change, leaving the transgender life and embracing life as the natal sex. This chapter describes reasons why some people choose to detransition, the hurdles to achieving detransition, and why we never seem to hear about those who do.

a. Hurdles to detransitioning

Detransition covers several aspects: social, legal and medical. These are the hurdles people face when they want to detransition.

Social detransition

Social transition and detransition involves changing the social aspects of one's life, such as wardrobe choices, hair style, pronouns and name to that of the opposite gender.

Legal detransition

All the legal documents that feature a person's name and sex, such as driver's license, social security card, birth certificate, passport need to be changed back.

Also, other secondary organizations and entities need to be alerted to the name change, such as financial institutions, landlord, employer and utilities.

Medical detransition

The process to medically detransition depends on what steps the individual took to alter his or her appearance.

Unfortunately, not all of what the surgeons do to change gender can be undone. Body parts that were sacrificed, reshaped, or removed will never function the original way again.

Women who decide to transition to male typically start by taking testosterone, the male hormone. Taking testosterone gives women facial hair and often renders them sterile. Women don't usually opt for what is called "bottom surgery," that is, the addition of male genitalia because it doesn't function very well. The few female-to-male people who have contacted me did not alter their genitalia.

They do what they can to eliminate female attributes. They have their breasts removed with a mastectomy to replicate the flat chest of a male. Some have a hysterectomy to remove the uterus and ovaries, but others don't and retain the option of having children, as seen in misleading headlines, "Man Having a Baby." It isn't a man—it's a woman who changed her appearance to present as a man and retained her God-given baby-making equipment.

To detransition, a woman stops taking testosterone which helps to re-feminize appearance, but any sterility it caused is permanent. If the woman had a hysterectomy, her reproductive parts are gone and cannot be restored, which means having biological children is not an option.

A challenge for the returning female is the beard which doesn't go away on its own. She'll need electrolysis treatments to remove the facial hair a single hair root at a time, which can be expensive and painful. Another question is what to do about the now-missing breasts. Adding breast implants can help mimic the appearance of the original ones. In making that decision, like all detransition decisions, it is up to the individual to weigh the pros and cons.

Men who transitioned to women and refashioned their male genitalia into a vagina (vaginoplasty) no longer have their original penis and testicles. When they wish to return to the male gender, one option is to have a phalloplasty procedure (the construction of a penis). But in practice, many men who detransition don't bother because it is expensive and risky. Besides, the resulting appendage does not function at the level of the original penis.

b. Reasons why people detransition

The reasons for detransitioning are many. Some people go back to their innate sex after a suicide attempt. Some simply conclude, "It just wasn't for me." Some have said it was too difficult to play dress-up as the opposite sex every day; it became too much trouble to keep the trans-life going. Some say they realized they were not real women and never would be. For others, medical problems caused by the surgery spark the desire to detransition. Whichever route they take to get there, from the stories I've heard many who reach the decision to detransition with a certainty and clarity that has been absent throughout their life. However difficult their lives have been, the stress distills a fundamental truth: we are created male and female and adopting an opposite sex identity is a futile pursuit.

For me, it was learning about the psychological factors that can cause someone to wrongly identify as a transgender. Early childhood sexual abuse is the leading cause reported to me, but there are often other factors. Studies have shown a multitude of other disorders coexist among transgender people and that experiences other than abuse can cause gender identity difficulty.

My eyes were opened when I entered a Certificate Study Program in the late 1980s that included courses in psychology pertaining to destructive behaviors and addictions. I started to realize the transgender condition could be a developmental disorder that evolved over time, like the formation of destructive behaviors, and not something innate at birth.

Like many of the 20% or so who report regret after surgical gender change, I first needed to come to terms with the truth that no amount of surgery or hormones can ever change innate, biological sex. Armed with the factual knowledge that my sex—male—had never changed, I started to take steps to detransition.

c. Why detransition isn't widely known

Sex change regret is more common than people know, but that fact is a well-kept secret. No one likes to admit they made a mistake and regretting gender change is a huge one. Resources are few and backlash from trans activists is plentiful, as Eric shared earlier:

> *I'm trying to come out as a regretter, and I'm finding the community backlash to be difficult and the lack of medical support to be troubling.*

Transgender people who wish to go back to their birth gender are marginalized and ostracized by members of the outspoken activists. The same people and online groups which embraced the person through their gender change will brand them as a traitor to the cause for going back. Where online friends once abounded, trolls will appear, and they are notoriously vicious. People considering detransition learn quickly not to confide in their former friends and supporters.

The surgeons who were so supportive in the patient's original transition (and benefitted financially from it) are suddenly and strangely tone deaf when someone has doubts afterward. As my contacts have reported, the surgeons say they have never heard of anyone who regretted surgery: "You're the first I've ever heard of." Then, the surgeons deflect blame back onto the patient, suggesting that it's the patient's fault: "You should have thought more carefully before having surgery." In my view, it's the *surgeon* who should have thought more carefully before *performing* the operation.

People who make the courageous decision to go back to living as their birth gender just want to maintain a low profile. They quickly decide that their top priorities are protecting themselves and their family members from attack and keeping a job. I understand. I've told my story publicly and been the target of negative trolling and outright fabrications about me. It hasn't been pretty.

Another reason that regret is not widely known is that left-leaning media aren't looking to publish stories that go against the politically-correct, all-pervasive narrative which says, "All gender changers are happy." No journalist who wishes to keep his or her career on track is going to seek out story lines about sex change regret.

An illustration of this is the case of Katie Herzog, a writer for the liberal outlet, *The Stranger*. Her piece, "The Detransitioners: They Were Transgender, Until They

Weren't,"[35] contained several personal accounts, was balanced and well-researched. But the police of political correctness—other liberal news writers and trans activists—quickly pounced on Herzog, loudly objecting to her article and trashing her personally for exposing the truth that people regret gender change.

[35] Herzog K., The Detransitioners: They Were Transgender, Until They Weren't, *The Stranger*, June 28, 2017, accessed on May 4, 2018, https://www.thestranger.com/features/2017/06/28/25252342/the-detransitioners-they-were-transgender-until-they-werent

38 Medical Realities of Sex Change

A physician who works with intersex and transgender patients wrote me this startling whistle-blower letter in April 2013:

> *Any physician worthy of his degree must treat ONLY with the Hippocratic Oath. First do no harm.* ***In this regard, we have willfully failed.***
> - *There is no female brain in the wrong male body*
> - *Current studies do not support the transsexual condition*
> - *Nor do the current studies support the Harry Benjamin Syndrome.*
>
> *Please don't mention my name. You would be surprised at the hostility of transsexual persons against physicians. I really do think that lots of physicians are very intimidated by them. The patients use the physicians and the physicians use the patients. It is deplorable. We have failed those with gender identity problems miserably.*

I have taken much time over the last 20 years to study, review and slowly start to understand that gender reassignment surgery is mostly unnecessary and often reckless as a treatment for gender disorders. As the physician above said, the gender specialists have willfully failed "to do no harm." The emails I continue to receive validate that view and, in this chapter, we'll look at how gender specialists use research to turn a blind eye to the harm done by sex change.

a. Research shows they're happy, right?

Most of the research studies that ask patients if their lives have improved after surgery have one, or several fatal flaws, the easiest of which to spot are: a significant percentage of patients aren't included (drop-out rate), participants are selected in a way that biases the results (selection bias) and the follow-up occurs too soon after surgery.

Follow up period too short

Most post-op transitioners *are* happy in the first year or two but check back with them after 5 or 10 years and the number of those dissatisfied with the trans life has increased. I've heard from people as far out as 30 years post-op who want to detransition. One researcher calls the first year "the honeymoon period," but I think the honeymoon can last several years:

> This one-year period [post-op] is often called the honeymoon period and does not present a representative picture of the long-term emotional and psychological status.[36]

[36] Cuypere, Griet & Elaut, Els & Heylens, Gunter & Maele, Georges & Selvaggi, Gennaro & T'Sjoen, Guy & Rubens, Robert , Bob & Hoebeke, Piet & Monstrey, Stan. (2006). Long-term follow-up: Psychosocial outcome of Belgian transsexuals after sex reassignment surgery. Sexologies. 15. 126-133. 10.1016/j.sexol.2006.04.002.

Selection bias and drop-out rate

I read studies that report high levels of happiness among those who undergo gender transition. But upon closer inspection it is quickly clear that a high percentage of the original patients aren't included. The people can't be located, or they don't want to participate. The claims of post-op happiness are based on only the ones the ones who agree to participate, which is a small, non-representative percentage of the total.

A recent example is found in the misleading NBC News headline, "Gender-affirming surgery 'significantly improves quality of life,' study says / Approximately 75 percent of transgender women showed an improved quality of life after surgery, a study out of Germany found."[37]

But reading the study shows that NBC News was parroting the overblown claims championed in the researchers' self-congratulatory press release while ignoring the study's extremely high drop-out rate:

> Of a total number of 610 male to female transgender who underwent GRS [Gender Reassignment Surgery] at the Department of Urology, University Hospital Essen between 1995 and 2015 [557 of the 610 were invited to

---

[37] Guillen Matheus V, Gender-affirming surgery 'significantly improves quality of life,' study says / Approximately 75 percent of transgender women showed an improved quality of life after surgery, a study out of Germany found., April 11, 2018, https://www.nbcnews.com/feature/nbc-out/gender-affirming-surgery-significantly-improves-quality-life-study-says-n862361

participate] a final sample of 156
individuals...could be surveyed.[38]

That's a drop-out rate of 72 percent! Three hundred and ninety-nine (399) people declined to participate, most for unknown reasons, so the researchers made their claims based on 156 people who agreed to participate. This is selection bias and leads to faulty conclusions.

What jumps out to me is that the "improved quality of life (Q of L)" touted by the researchers and by the media was experienced by only 117 (75% of 156) people out of 557 who were invited to participate, a paltry 21% of the total. The only conclusion that can be confidently drawn from this research is that 21% reported satisfaction.

A potentially explosive nugget in this report that the researchers ignored completely is that 1 in 4 (39 people) of the participants reported *dissatisfaction* or lower quality of life (Q of L) with GRS results. Twenty-five percent (25%) regret rate reported in a trans-friendly study is an unintended disclosure with huge ramifications. It seriously questions the common myth spread by activists that GRS regret is rare.

What happened to the 399 people who dropped out? The reasons for not including them are given as: No response (210), Post undeliverable (168), Deceased (14), Not interested (7). It makes sense to me that depressed, remorseful people are not likely to respond or don't want to be found. But, what if they, too, are dissatisfied? Including some portion of them as regretters would boost

[38] European Association of Urology press release, First accurate data showing that male to female transgender surgery can lead to a better life, March 17, 2018, accessed on August 1, 2018 at http://uroweb.org/wp-content/uploads/first-accurate-data-showing-that-male-to-female-transgender-surgery-can-lead-to-a-better-life.pdf

the regret rate from the reported 25% to *as much as 79%,* as seen in the following pictorial representation.

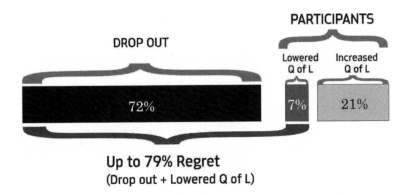

PARTICIPANTS

DROP OUT

Lowered Q of L

Increased Q of L

72%

7%

21%

Up to 79% Regret
(Drop out + Lowered Q of L)

The press release quotes an independent university professor, Jens Sønksen (University of Copenhagen), who concedes "the study suffered from a high drop-out rate," but nevertheless says, "This is probably the best view of quality of life in after sex-reassignment that we have."

The best view they have, when 7 out of 10 patients disappeared from the study? Could it be that some of those missing patients are among the many hundreds who have contacted me, expressing deep regret over their surgery? Would any other major surgery be so aggressively pursued when the research is so severely lacking? Perhaps it is time for researchers to start talking to my contacts, if they're serious about getting an accurate picture of post-surgery quality of life.

b. It's not science, it's an experiment

Most regretters come to understand it is categorically impossible to achieve a sex change, biologically, scientifically, or surgically. A change of sex is only a hypothesis and the recommended treatment isn't based on controlled, randomized long-term scientific research; the patients are unknowingly and innocently corralled in an experimental treatment whose results are not accurately tracked.

Unfortunately, this experiment is being performed on children as well as adults. When the reality sets in—and it may take 5 to 15 years to set in—regret and depression follow. The regretters see, through the clarified vision afforded by hindsight, that undergoing sex change was a big mistake with unimaginable, unwanted, serious and lifelong, irreversible consequences.

Many esteemed endocrinologists, surgeons, other medical doctors and advocates for gender change have failed miserably for over 50 years to prove that gender change provides long-term resolution or a full life of gender bliss.

A task force commissioned by the American Psychiatric Association (APA) couldn't find any evidence. It did a review of the literature on the treatment of gender identity disorder in 2012 and stated: "The quality of evidence pertaining to most aspects of treatment in all subgroups was determined to be low..."[39] How can it be that no one over the last 50 years has been able to fashion a study with a high quality of scientific evidence that sex change works as a treatment?

In 2004, the Aggressive Research Intelligence Facility (ARIF) at University of Birmingham, under the guidance of Dr. Chris Hyde, conducted a review of more than 100 international medical studies of post-operative

---

[39] Byne W1, Bradley SJ, Coleman E, Eyler AE, Green R, Menvielle EJ, Meyer-Bahlburg HF, Pleak RR, Tompkins DA; "Report of the American Psychiatric Association Task Force on Treatment of Gender Identity Disorder", Arch Sex Behav. 2012 Aug;41(4):759-96. doi: 10.1007/s10508-012-9975-x, accessed on August 14, 2018 at http://www.ncbi.nlm.nih.gov/pubmed/22736225

transsexuals and found "no robust scientific evidence that gender reassignment surgery is clinically effective."[40]

The APA says that they can make treatment recommendations based on clinical consensus. But "clinical consensus" is code for the opinion of doctors who run gender clinics and are pre-disposed to confirm their bias. The gender specialists often insist they personally have never had anyone regret. But they don't know because they don't follow up with their patients. People with regret, depression and shame generally don't go back to their original providers with news of regret, especially when many years have passed. Those few who do tell me that the surgeon says it's the patient's fault—they should have made a better decision!

That's a travesty. And worse, that travesty has been known since at least the 1970s, when one of the foremost practitioners sounded the alarm.

c. Circa 1970s whistleblower—Ihlenfeld

One of the first whistleblowers on the failure of sex change came from an unlikely source within the gender specialist medical community—Dr. Harry Benjamin's private clinic. Dr. Harry Benjamin was a strong early advocate for cross-sex hormone therapy and gender reassignment surgery who operated a private clinic for transsexuals.

Benjamin's trusted colleague, endocrinologist Charles Ihlenfeld administered hormone therapy to some 500 transgender people over a period of six years at Benjamin's clinic—until he became concerned about the outcomes.

---

[40] Batty, D., Sex changes are not effective, say researchers, *The Guardian*, 30 Jul 2004, accessed on August 14, 2018 at
http://www.theguardian.com/society/2004/jul/30/health.mentalhealth

"There is too much unhappiness among people who have the surgery," he said. "Too many of them end as suicides. 80% who want to change their sex shouldn't do it." But even for the 20% he thought might be good candidates for it, sex change is by no means a solution to life's problems. (It's interesting that Ihlenfeld's 20% estimate based on his clinical experience matches so closely to the 21% satisfied respondents in the 2018 study we discussed earlier.)

Ihlenfeld thinks of sex change more as a kind of reprieve. "It buys maybe 10 or 15 years of a happier life," he said. But I would say the reprieve is not worth it. After my sex change I had a reprieve of seven or eight years, then what? I was worse off than before. I looked like a woman—my legal documents identified me as a woman—yet I found that at the end of the "reprieve" I wanted to be a man every bit as passionately as I had once yearned to be a woman.

Based on his experience treating 500 transgender patients, Dr. Ihlenfeld concluded that the desire to change genders most likely stemmed from powerful psychological factors:

> "Whatever surgery did, it did not fulfill a basic yearning for something that is difficult to define. This goes along with the idea that we are trying to treat superficially something that is much deeper."[41]

Dr. Ihlenfeld left endocrinology in 1975 to begin a psychiatry residency so he could deliver the psychological help transgender people need.

In 2011, while writing my book, *Paper Genders*, I was curious and called Dr. Ihlenfeld to ask if anything had

---

[41] *Transgender Subjectivities: A Clinician's Guide*, (ed: Leli, U., and Drescher, J.) The Haworth Medical Press, an imprint of The Haworth Press, Inc., 2004, p. 151

changed his mind about the remarks he made in 1979. Ihlenfeld was polite to me on the phone and quickly said that no, nothing had changed his mind. It is interesting in today's atmosphere of political correctness that Dr. Ihlenfeld, a homosexual, holds the view that gender reassignment surgery isn't the answer to alleviate the psychological factors that drive many with the compulsion to change genders. I appreciate his honest, clinical evaluation of the evidence and refusal to bend the medical results to fit a political viewpoint.

Dr. Ihlenfeld thoughts from the 1970s are mirrored in the 2004 University of Birmingham review of over 100 studies:

> "While no doubt great care is taken to ensure appropriate patients undergo gender reassignment, there is still a large number of people who have had the surgery but remain traumatized to the point of committing suicide."[42]

Despite the same observations being made across 30 years, patient and provider expectations of surgical solutions for gender dysphoria are far too high, and the unforeseen consequences bring too many patients to the depths of despair. Yet, the APA and WPATH do nothing to encourage investigation into how and why.

d. Gender Dysphoria: Born that way?

Gender dysphoria is not the result of a brain hormone wash or chromosome disorders or someone having been born with the brain of the opposite gender. Studies say, "It may be caused by this in the brain" or "It may be this gene

---

[42] Batty, D., Sex changes are not effective, say researchers, op.cit.

in the DNA" but the research is far from finding—much less proving—any biological cause.

On the other hand, overwhelming evidence of life trauma is on full view in the emails I receive. Gender confusion and distress develop most often early in life from trauma, grief, stress, feelings of abandonment, or deep loss or feelings of abuse, even if the abuse didn't exist.

A simple explanation of dysphoria is that it is the opposite of euphoria. Instead of intense excitement and happiness, the person with dysphoria is filled with sadness, despair and intense unease about their internal sense of gender not matching their biological sex.

To the person drowning in pain, changing genders looks like a life preserver. They feel if they change genders, the pain will go away. But as so many stories demonstrate, the pain lingers and even worsens, because early life trauma has not been addressed. Depression and suicidality are not resolved by changing gender.

e. Depression and suicide

Over 40% of transgender adults attempt suicide at some time, even after changing their sex.[43] As the research shows, a high percentage of this population has clinical depression, the undisputed leading cause of suicide.[44]

This was dramatically illustrated in a nationwide survey of Swedes who obtained sex-reassignment surgery within a culture strongly supportive of the transgender

---

[43] Grant, JM. Ph.D., Mottet, LA. J.D., Tanis, J, D.Min, "Injustice at Every Turn: A Report of the National Transgender Discrimination Survey", 2016, accessed on August 14, 2018 at https://transequality.org/sites/default/files/docs/resources/NTDS_Report.pdf

[44] According to suicide.org, over 90% of people who commit suicide are suffering from depression.

population. It has an advantage other studies do not—in Sweden's system of national health care, they obtained many decades of comprehensive, individualized health records for the entire population. These records are available for group analysis and study.

That study generated very concerning results: 10 to 15 years after surgical reassignment, the suicide rate rose to *twenty times* that of comparable (non-transgender) peers.

The study's conclusion states:

> "Persons with transsexualism, after sex reassignment, have considerably higher risks for mortality, suicidal behavior, and psychiatric morbidity [diseased state] than the general population. Our findings suggest that sex reassignment, although alleviating gender dysphoria, may not suffice as treatment for transsexualism." [45]

Sex change regret has no boundaries of male or female, race, religion or nationality, or length of time after surgery as this letter from a regretter shows.

> *Hi Walt,*
>
> *I live outside the US but like you I am another in the growing list of people who have had SRS and have come to regret it years later.*
>
> *I have visited your website [sexchangeregret.com] and thank you for your dedication in telling your story and getting the truth*

[45] Dhejne C1, Lichtenstein P, Boman M, Johansson AL, Långström N, Landén M., "Long-term follow-up of transsexual persons undergoing sex reassignment surgery: cohort study in Sweden.", PLoS One. 2011 Feb 22;6(2):e16885. doi: 10.1371/journal.pone.0016885., accessed on July 11, 2018 at http://www.ncbi.nlm.nih.gov/pubmed/21364939

*out. The Swedish study you have on your website is
a real note of caution.*
Take care.

f. Diagnose and treat comorbid disorders first

According to a multitude of studies[46], a high rate of those
who request a change of gender are suffering from
comorbid, or co-existing, mental disorders that have not
been properly diagnosed or treated. The co-existing
disorders include anxiety, depression, obsessive
compulsive disorder, dissociative disorder, bipolar
disorder, schizophrenia, personality disorder, narcissism,
separation anxiety, and body dysmorphic disorder.

Many of these disorders manifest with the desire to
change gender. In other words, a patient will feel distress
with their gender and want to change it, but some other
disorder is causing the feelings. After proper diagnosis and
treatment for the comorbid disorder, the patient's feelings
of gender distress go away.

The importance of getting this right has lifelong
ramifications for the patient because sex change
procedures are not fully reversible. If a person still feels
gender dysphoric after surgery, then obviously sex change
didn't fix it and was the wrong treatment. The symptoms
must have some other cause. For the patient living this
horrible nightmare, the devastating realization that their
treatment has only added to their problems can lead to
what Dr. Ihlenfeld observed: "Too many of them [people
who have the surgery] end as suicides."

---

[46] Six studies showing the prevalence of comorbid disorders are listed in the
following section, "Comorbid studies."

A prudent diagnosis and treatment plan would seek to eliminate the comorbid disorders as a possible cause *before* recommending radical surgery. It seems irresponsible to remove perfectly good body parts as the first step in treatment rather than checking thoroughly for the presence of other contributing factors and treating them to see if the dysphoria dissipates.

I am continually shocked by the number of people who write me to say that, even though they suffered from a known mental disorder for years, their gender specialists ignore it and fast-track them to surgery. I naturally wondered how prevalent comorbid disorders were among people with gender dysphoria and did some research. I found it's an astonishing number, as you will see in the following scientific studies

g. Comorbid studies

The following studies provide irrefutable evidence that people with gender dysphoria overwhelmingly suffer from a variety of comorbid, or co-existing, mental disorders.

> *Note: "Axis I" comorbid disorders referenced in these studies include anxiety, depression, obsessive compulsive, dissociative disorder, bipolar, schizophrenia, personality disorder, narcissism, separation anxiety, and body dysmorphic disorder.*

1. An August 2014 study concluded: "Consistent with most earlier researches, the majority of patients with gender dysphoria had psychiatric Axis I comorbidity."

   62.7% of those diagnosed with gender dysphoria suffer from psychiatric Axis I comorbid disorders, or co-existing mental illness. Fifty-seven (62.7%) patients had at least one psychiatric comorbidity.

Major depressive disorder (33.7%), specific phobia (20.5%), and adjustment disorder (15.7%) were the three most prevalent disorders.[47]

2. "90 percent of these diverse patients had at least one other significant form of psychopathology" reported Case Western Reserve University in a 2009 study of transgender outcomes at their clinic. Nine out of the last ten patients were suffering from a mental illness that gender surgery did not alleviate.[48]

The researchers had some stern words for gender specialists:

"Emphasis on civil rights is not a substitute for the recognition and treatment of associated psychopathology. Gender identity specialists, unlike the media, need to be concerned about the majority of patients, not just the ones who are apparently functioning well in transition."

3. A 2003 Dutch survey of board-certified Dutch psychiatrists found that 61%... (359 people) had other psychiatric disorders and illnesses, notably

---

[47] Azadeh Mazaheri Meybodi, Ahmad Hajebi, and Atefeh Ghanbari Jolfaei, "Psychiatric Axis I Comorbidities among Patients with Gender Dysphoria," *Psychiatry Journal*, vol. 2014, Article ID 971814, 5 pages, 2014, accessed on May 22, 2018 at https://doi.org/10.1155/2014/971814.

[48] Levine SB, Solomon A., Meanings and political implications of "psychopathology" in a gender identity clinic: a report of 10 cases., J Sex Marital Ther. 2009;35(1):40-57, accessed on July 29, 2018 at https://www.ncbi.nlm.nih.gov/pubmed/19105079

personality, mood, dissociative, and psychotic disorders.[49]

4. A 2013 University of Louisville, KY study of 351 transgender individuals found that the rates of depression and anxiety symptoms within the study "far surpass the rates of those for the general population." About half had depressive symptoms and more than 40% had symptoms of anxiety.[50]

5. A 2005 Switzerland University Hospital study of a cross-sectional sample of 31 patients treated for GID showed 39% fulfilled the criteria for current Axis I disorder and 71% for current and/or lifetime Axis I diagnosis.[51]

6. A 2014 multi-center survey in four European countries of 305 persons diagnosed with GID found people with gender identity disorder show more psychiatric problems than the general population. "In 38% of the individuals with gender identity disorder a current DSM-IV-TR Axis I diagnosis was found, mainly affective disorders and anxiety

---

[49] Campo J, Nijman H, Merckelbach H, Evers C. Psychiatric comorbidity of gender identity disorders: a survey among Dutch psychiatrists. Am J Psychiatry 2003;160:1332-6, accessed on July 30, 2018 at https://www.ncbi.nlm.nih.gov/pubmed/12832250

[50] Budge S.L., Adelson J.L., Howard K.A. Anxiety and depression in transgender individuals: The roles of transition status, loss, social support, and coping. J. Consul. Clin. Psychol. 2013;81:545. doi: 10.1037/a0031774, accessed on July 30, 2018 at https://www.ncbi.nlm.nih.gov/pubmed/23398495

[51] Hepp U, Kraemer B, Schnyder U, Miller N, Delsignore A. Psychiatric comorbidity in gender identity disorder. J Psychosom Res. 2005;58:259–61, accessed on July 30, 2018 at https://www.ncbi.nlm.nih.gov/pubmed/15865950

disorders. Furthermore, almost 70% had a current and lifetime diagnosis."[52]

The presence of mental disorders has monumental implications for transgender treatment and should be taken seriously. One reason is because of the strong association between some psychiatric disorders and suicide. The other is that treatment for the other mental disorders can alleviate the gender dysphoria. Misdiagnosing the problem and treating people who have psychiatric disorders with cross-sex hormones and surgery seems to me to be a formula for producing future regret and suicide.

I continue to receive emails from people post-op who are despondent and suicidal. Surgery didn't fix their distress, they seek answers as to why, and eventually they realize they suffer from some psychiatric or psychological issue that their gender specialists ignored.

---

[52] Heylens G, Verroken C, De Cock S et al, (2014), Effects of different steps in gender reassignment therapy on psychopathology: a prospective study of persons with a gender identity disorder, J Sex Med 11:119–126, Vol. 204, Issue 2 February 2014, pp. 151-156, accessed July 30, 2018 at https://doi.org/10.1192/bjp.bp.112.121954

39 Medical Associations Turn Political: APA and WPATH

a. DSM, the official handbook from the American Psychiatric Association (APA)

The American Psychiatric Association (APA) produces the official authoritative guide to the *diagnosis* of mental disorders used by health care professionals in the United States and much of the world, *The Diagnostic and Statistical Manual of Mental Disorders (DSM)*. The *DSM* contains descriptions, symptoms, and other criteria for diagnosing mental disorders, but is not the place for guidelines regarding treatment.[53] (The guidelines for treatment, called the standards of care (SOC), are published by a separate group and discussed in the next section).

An interesting thing happened in the latest revision. The Fifth Edition (*DSM-5*), published in 2013, drops "gender identity disorder" (GID) and adds a new condition called "gender dysphoria" (GD).

---

[53] APA website, "*DSM-5*: Frequently Asked Questions", accessed July 31, 2018 at https://www.psychiatry.org/psychiatrists/practice/dsm/feedback-and-questions/frequently-asked-questions

The intent behind the change is to destigmatize transgender behaviors by removing the word "disorder." But insurance reimbursement depends on having a diagnosable condition in the *DSM*. "Gender dysphoria" is the compromise to fulfill both objectives. Transgender individuals are no longer diagnosed with a mental condition unless they *feel distress* at the mismatch between their identities and their bodies.[54] Then the diagnosis is gender dysphoria.

The name change did not help reduce the number of people who have regrets or attempt suicide. The new name has not resolved what causes the desire to identify as transgender. This change demonstrates that the APA puts advocacy above scientific pursuit.

The APA itself says in an article on their website that they have increased their advocacy:

> APA and other groups have increased their advocacy on behalf of transgender people as well. In 2008, APA's Council of Representatives adopted its Resolution on Transgender, Gender Identity and Gender Expression Nondiscrimination to support full equality and "the legal and social recognition of transgender individuals consistent with their gender identity and expression."[55]

What traditionally are viewed as scientific and professional organizations now advocate for legal rights. I don't think the public realizes to what extent the

---

[54] Russo F., "Where Transgender Is No Longer a Diagnosis", *Scientific American*, January 6, 2017, accessed on July 30, 2018 at https://www.scientificamerican.com/article/where-transgender-is-no-longer-a-diagnosis/

[55] Glicksman, E., "Transgender today", *Monitor on Psychology*, April 2013, Vol 44, No. 4, accessed on July 30, 2018 at http://www.apa.org/monitor/2013/04/transgender.aspx

corruption affects the vulnerable population of people suffering with strong feelings of gender dysphoria.

Dr. Corradi of Case Western says of the DSM-5, "[R]ather than providing a scientific validation of the transgender agenda, the APA's action was a remarkable abrogation of professional responsibility in the interest of political correctness."[56]

Next, we'll see how the changes in the latest standards of care (SOC-7) work in tandem with the DSM-5 to stifle much-needed research and limit treatment options for this vulnerable population.

b. Standards of Care (SOC) by WPATH

For the treatment of people who report having discomfort with their gender identity, The World Professional Association for Transgender Health (WPATH) develops guidelines for the medical community called the standards of care for transgender health, now in the seventh revision (SOC-7).[57]

The standards of care do not come with any requirement that they be followed. The standards advise that each patient's case is different, so the medical practitioners may, and should, adapt the protocols to the

[56] Corradi, RB, "Psychiatry Professor: 'Transgenderism' Is Mass Hysteria Similar To 1980s-Era Junk Science", *The Federalist*, November 17, 2016, accessed on August 15, 2018 at http://thefederalist.com/2016/11/17/psychiatry-professor-transgenderism-mass-hysteria-similar-1980s-era-junk-science/

[57] "Standards of Care for the Health of Transsexual, Transgender, and Gender Nonconforming People", published by WPATH is available at https://www.wpath.org/publications/soc

individual. The SOC refers to itself as "flexible clinical guidelines."

People think that because standards exist, people with gender dysphoria will be properly screened before undergoing the radical gender transition. Unfortunately, the overwhelming theme of the latest version of the standards is "affirmation." The role of clinical practitioners has been dumbed down to merely approving and affirming the client's self-diagnosis of gender dysphoria and helping the client toward, and through, transition.

The SOC ignores evidence GD can remit and calls counseling futile and unethical

Kenneth Zucker, long-time gender researcher and clinician, believes gender dysphoria can arise from a variety of causes, and that it's an oversimplification to assume transition is the best approach when someone is suffering from its effects.[58]

I agree completely. Gender dysphoria is a complex topic and the diverse group of patients have a wide range of motivations for wanting to change gender. Even though the topic has been studied for over 50 years, discovering the causes and best methods of treatment is still in its infancy.

But SOC-7 seeks to discourage research into the diverse sub-groups and causes of GD and ignores studies that say GD can go into remission. According to the Chair of one of the DSM-5 revision work groups:

> It is recognized that GD can remit in some cases (Marks et al. 2000); perhaps psychotherapy could

---

[58] Singal, J., 'You Should Watch the BBC's Controversial Documentary on the Gender-Dysphoria Researcher Kenneth Zucker (Updated)", *The Cut*, January 13, 2017, accessed on August 2, 2018 at https://www.thecut.com/ 2017/01/you-should-watch-the-bbcs-kenneth-zucker-documentary.html

facilitate such remission—or a reduction in GD symptoms, with greater congruence between gender identity and expression and assigned sex— in some subset of the diverse group of adults whose gender problems now qualify for a diagnosis of GD. **Unfortunately, these possibilities have not yet been investigated, and such investigations are strongly discouraged in the SOC-7** [emphasis added]. [59]

SOC-7 calls efforts to help adults with GD find greater acceptance and comfort with their biological sex futile and unethical. They base their conclusion on flimsy outdated evidence:

The citations allegedly demonstrating that such treatment efforts are "without success" **date from 30 to 50 years ago** [emphasis added] ... [60]

The SOC-7 references 30-year-old research to condemn contemporary counseling even though current research exists which shows that GD can remit.[61] Based on their commitment to advocacy, I suspect the authors of SOC-7 have carefully constructed wording to lay the foundation for banishing counseling from the standards in the future. WPATH has succeeded in making SOC-7 the prime authority on transgender health. The sad effects of publishing faulty conclusions based on outdated, refuted science are as extensive as they are destructive.

---

[59] Zucker, KJ, Lawrence, AA, Kreukels, BP, "Gender Dysphoria in Adults", The Annual Review of Clinical Psychology, 2016. 12:20.1–20.31, p. 21. doi: 10.1146/annurev-clinpsy-021815-093034

[60] Ibid.

[61] Ibid.

c. Chilling effects of APA and WPATH advocacy

Criminalizing counseling

Activists find it helpful to quote from the DSM and SOC to validate their arguments, such as in legal briefs when lobbying for legislation. Unfortunately, but understandably, no lawmaker will dig deeper to see that the basis of the supposedly valid conclusions, policy and recommendations is outdated, refuted studies, so they vote for harmful laws.

Several U.S. states have enacted legislation to punish counselors if they help adolescents and children under age eighteen with gender dysphoria become comfortable in their natal sex (which studies say most children will achieve). The crime is *child abuse*, which is a horrific criminal conviction with extreme punishment.

Not content with only imprisoning children in transgender land, advocates are pressuring for legislation to outlaw the counseling for adults, too. The Therapeutic Fraud Prevention Act, put forward in April 2017 in Congress, would expressly forbid mental health professionals from attempting to "change another individual's . . . gender identity." If it passes, it turns counselors into criminals if they help clients accept their physical sex. The difference from the laws targeting children is that in this case the clients are *adults*, who should be permitted to make counseling choices freely.

I've spoken with counselors who say the practical effect of such laws is that medical professionals will be very careful not to take people with gender dysphoria on as clients, because any topic but "affirming" can be said to violate the law. Explore the effects of childhood trauma? No, don't go there. Counseling might reveal the cause of gender discomfort and initiate an illegal conversation. Grief counseling? Ditto. Diagnose co-morbid disorders? Beware, you could lose your counseling license. In effect, counseling for gender dysphoric people for psychological issues will no longer be available, even if they request it.

The only counseling that remains legal under these draconian laws is affirmation and support of gender change. Counseling someone with gender issues for childhood trauma or co-morbid disorders is grounds for prosecution and loss of license to practice.

When it comes to withholding counseling, the advocate agenda wins, and the patients lose.

Punishing researchers

The advocacy of APA and WPATH has a chilling effect on scientific discovery. It emboldens advocates to stop any scientific pursuit which would poke holes through the politically correct narrative through censure, intimidation and defamation of the scientists who participate.

Just ask James Caspian, a psychotherapist who specializes in working with transgender people. Caspian noticed an increase in the number of transgender people were requesting reversal of their genital surgery and he was curious about it. He pursued an advanced degree with the intention of using this as the topic for his research. In September 2017, the United Kingdom's Bath Spa University turned down his application to conduct research on gender reassignment reversals. The university deemed the subject "potentially politically incorrect."[62] Caspian isn't a radical outsider; he is inside the

---

[62] Heyer, W., "University Refuses Research on Growing Numbers of Trans People Who Want to Go Back", *The Federalist*, October 4, 2018, accessed on July 31, 2018 at http://thefederalist.com/2017/10/04/university-refuses-research-growing-numbers-trans-people-want-go-back/

transgender medical community but that didn't protect him.

Another alarming example of how quickly gender professionals can fall from grace is Kenneth Zucker, a prominent gender specialist with impressive credentials: Chair of one of the DSM-5 revision work groups (2007-2013), prolific researcher, and Director of the Toronto Ontario Gender Identity Clinic. In 2015, the trans advocates smeared him in the court of public opinion and successfully pressured his employer into firing him based on false claims of hurting children.

John Whitehall, professor of pediatrics at Western Sydney University, wrote about Zucker after he learned about his dismissal. In his article, "Gender Dysphoria and the Fashion in Child Surgical Abuse," Whitehall wrote, "In fifty years I have not witnessed such a reluctance to express an opinion among my colleagues."[63] Exhibiting scientific curiosity, asking questions, following the evidence, constructing research projects—if any of these threaten transgender ideology or its politically-correct narrative—these are deemed radical acts and severely punished.

---

[63] Whitehall, J, Gender dysphoria and the fashion in child surgical abuse [online]. Quadrant, Vol. 60, No. 12, Dec 2016: 23-33.
https://search.informit.com.au/documentSummary;dn=483076857065690;
res=IELLCC

40 Concluding Remarks

Each gut-wrenching story in this book represents testimonial proof that too many gender therapists are failing miserably to prevent sex change regret. The stories showcase the recklessness of gender therapists in quickly diagnosing gender dysphoria, refusing to diagnose and treat the deeper underlying comorbid disorders, and rushing patients to transition. Regrettable outcomes are the direct result. Unless the transgender health medical associations acknowledge the failures and change the treatment protocols, many more distressed people will be caught up in inappropriate and unnecessary cross-gender hormone therapies and surgeries, which will result in more regrettable outcomes, including suicide.

Real people with real stories filled with pain and consequences are a chilling reminder of the madness of changing genders and the hell that awaits those who live the trans life. Even transgender activist Kyle Scanlon sadly committed suicide and the Hollywood personality Alexis Arquette, after living the transgender life, called changing genders "bullshit."

If you are struggling with living life in the trans world, please understand you can reclaim your lost life; the door is open for you. Your story can be an inspiration for others, too. Join me and the growing chorus of survivors who detransitioned and now sing, "No more trans life for me."

One last email from October 4, 2018, from Laura, former female-to-male, shows why my work is important.

> *Hi, Walt, I'm sure you don't remember my email, but I emailed you about two years ago shortly after I had left the transgender lifestyle to follow Christ...*
>
> *Over the last two years God has peeled away the layers of the onion and I have now come to understand the point you have been making for so long, that these alternate identities are the result of trauma... I just wanted you to know that. Maybe to encourage you that even if people say you are wrong, maybe they just don't see it yet. I wasn't ready to face it all then. It took time, but God is faithful, and He has healed the pain of my past...*
>
> *Thank you for your courage, you are my hero, but I recognize it is Jesus Christ. But still, thank you for speaking out and standing alone for so long. You paved the way for many more coming behind you. There is a revival among transgenders beginning.*
>
> *May the Lord bless you richly.*
> *Laura P.*

You can surrender your life to your feelings and desires.
You can surrender your life to the trans ideology.
Or you can surrender your life to Christ and find healing for your soul.

I chose Christ and He led me out into a sane, fulfilled and genuine life, to be the man He created me to be.
–Walt Heyer

Glossary *and* Terminology

Language on this topic keeps changing, with new terms and definitions replacing the former at a hectic clip. Words that were widely used and noncontroversial not so long ago are now considered "transphobic" and offensive.

With terms changing so frequently, it is easy to give offense where none is intended, much less desired. The words used in this book by the people themselves to describe their experiences vary tremendously, and to be true to their stories I have preserved their words, even when they were out-of-date or out-of-fashion. The key is to keep your eye on the story, and not pay heed to semantic fashions or fads.

Sex vs. gender

Sex has two possibilities: male or female, which are based on physical, biological attributes, such as chromosomes and genitalia related to human reproduction. Sex does not change in humans; male and female are two halves of one reproductive whole.

Gender is a self-perception based in a person's beliefs and has many possibilities—male, female, "other" or "fluid." In this book, I left the terms as my contacts used them when I quote from conversations, but when I am writing, "sex" means being male or female, while "gender" refers to a person's subjective self-perception of masculine or feminine.

What the surgery is called

In the 1980s, the surgical procedure to refashion the genitalia to appear like that of the opposite sex was called a sex change. Since then it gone through many labels, such as sex reassignment surgery (SRS), gender reassignment surgery, gender affirming surgery and gender confirmation surgery. In this book, these terms are used interchangeably.

MTF and FTM

- MTF is shorthand for born male, going to female.
- FTM is shorthand for born female, going to male.

MTF and FTM indicate the direction the person intends to go, regardless of where they are in the process.

Gender Identity Disorder (GID) vs. Gender Dysphoria (GD)

Both terms refer to a difference between one's experienced/expressed gender and anatomical sex, and significant distress or problems functioning.[64]

- Gender Identity Disorder (GID) appeared in the DSM-4 and was dropped in DSM-5.
- Gender Dysphoria (GD) was added in DSM-5.

In this book, the terms are used interchangeably.

---

[64] https://www.psychiatry.org/patients-families/gender-dysphoria/what-is-gender-dysphoria accessed on June 1, 2018

Sexual orientation and gender identity

Gender identity has nothing to do with sexual orientation. A person who identifies as the opposite sex can have any of the full range of sexual attractions: asexual (none), homosexual, bisexual or heterosexual.

Transgender

The word "transgender" is used as an umbrella term to cover a wide range of cross-sex expression. A few of the more common ones are listed here.

Drag queens—Largely homosexual, very flamboyant, over-the-top imitators of women who are featured prominently in gay pride parades.

Crossdressers—Usually heterosexual men who will not be leading a gay pride parade. They stay out of sight, secretly wearing women's clothing, make-up and jewelry in their homes or motel rooms, not wanting to be discovered.

Transvestites—Typically men who cross dress as women, they get some gratification from wearing women's clothing and will often mingle in bars and restaurants under the cover of darkness. For transvestites, dressing up was never about being a woman.

Autogynepheliacs—Usually men who cross dress, look in the mirror and fall in love with and are sexually aroused by the image of themselves dressed as a woman. Many suggest this is a sex-fueled fetish.

Gender queer and fluid—People who experiment back and forth with changing genders or who exhibit non-traditional gender expression. Gaining popularity among teens and young adults.

Transsexual (TS)—A person who underwent genital surgery.

Psychologically troubled—These individuals may be of either sex and suffer unresolved mental illness that manifests as distress over one's perceived gender not matching their sex and acting out as the other sex. After gender reassignment surgery, the psychological illness still exists and needs to be addressed. Alternatively, comprehensive counseling for the psychological issues often resolves the gender dysphoria so that gender reassignment surgery is no longer desired.

DSM

The American Psychiatric Association's (APA) official guide for diagnosing and treating psychiatric disorders, the *Diagnostic and Statistical Manual of Mental Disorders (DSM)*, now in its fifth edition (DSM-5).

SOC

Standards of care for transgender health, now in the seventh revision (SOC-7). Developed by The World Professional Association for Transgender Health (WPATH).

Appendix. Resources

For detransition

Because the World Professional Association for Transgender Health (WPATH), offers no resources for detransitioning, all of us detransitioners cobble together our own treatment plan and medical team through trial and error. We search the internet for other detransitioners and learn from their journey.

Here are some of those resources to get you started with quotes from their online descriptions.

Guide on Raging Stars, guideonragingstars.tumblr.com

Blog by Cari Stella, resource for FTM detransitioners

Cari Stella conducted a survey on her blog in 2016 of previously dysphoric women who have either stopped their transition or taken steps to reverse it. Within the short span of two weeks, 203 women responded.

The results are available at:

http://guideonragingstars.tumblr.com/post/1498777061 75/female-detransition-and-reidentification-survey

GenderCriticalResources.com

A wiki to share gender critical ideas and resources.
This may include the following:
- People opposed to or questioning the Doctrine of Gender Identity and the transgender movement

- People concerned by people they love and care for getting involved in the transgender movement, starting transition or having transitioned
- People who have become involved in the transgender movement and are concerned by where this will lead them or the cult-like nature of the transgender movement.

For understanding the issue

When Harry Became Sally:
Responding to the Transgender Moment

by Ryan T. Anderson (2018)

Can a boy be "trapped" in a girl's body? Can modern medicine "reassign" sex? Is our sex "assigned" to us in the first place? What is the most loving response to a person experiencing a conflicted sense of gender? What should our law say on matters of "gender identity"?

When Harry Became Sally provides thoughtful answers to questions arising from our transgender moment. Drawing on the best insights from biology, psychology, and philosophy, Ryan Anderson offers a nuanced view of human embodiment, a balanced approach to public policy on gender identity, and a sober assessment of the human costs of getting human nature wrong.

God and the Transgender Debate

by Andrew T. Walker (2017)

This warm, faithful and careful book helps Christians understand what the Bible says about gender identity. It will help us to engage lovingly, thoughtfully and faithfully with one of the most explosive cultural discussions of our day.

Resources: Gender and Sexuality Issues

The Minnesota Family Council website, mfc.org, includes links to additional resources grouped into these categories:

- Christian Response to the Transgenderism Movement
- The Absurdity of the Transgenderism Movement
- Transgenderism Impacting Your Child

"Boys Girls Other"

By Glenn T. Stanton

Making Sense of the Confusing New World of Gender Identity, Commissioned by Family First New Zealand, 2015

Available at www.familyfirst.org.nz

Gender Ideology Harms Children

American College of Pediatricians Position Statement, updated September 2017.

An excerpt:

The American College of Pediatricians urges healthcare professionals, educators and legislators to reject all policies that condition children to accept as normal a life of chemical and surgical impersonation of the opposite sex. Facts – not ideology – determine reality.

Available at:

www.acpeds.org/the-college-speaks/position-statements/gender-ideology-harms-children

Sexuality and Gender—Findings from the Biological, Psychological, and Social Sciences

by Lawrence S. Mayer, Paul R. McHugh (2016)

An excerpt:

This report presents a careful summary and an up-to-date explanation of research—from the biological, psychological, and social sciences— related to sexual orientation and gender identity. It is offered in the hope that such an exposition can contribute to our capacity as physicians, scientists, and citizens to address health issues faced by LGBT populations within our society.

Available at www.thenewatlantis.com

For parents

4thWaveNow.com

A community of parents and others concerned about the medicalization of gender-atypical youth and rapid-onset gender dysphoria (ROGD)

TransgenderTrend.com

Parents questioning the trans narrative:

We are a group of parents based in the UK, who are concerned about the current trend to diagnose 'gender non-conforming' children as transgender. We reject current conservative, reactionary, religious-fundamentalist views about sexuality and we have no political affiliation. We are also concerned about legislation which places transgender rights above the right to safety for girls and young women in public bathrooms and changing rooms.

We come from diverse backgrounds, some with expertise in child development and psychology, some who themselves were extreme gender non-conforming children and adolescents, some whose own children have self-diagnosed as 'trans' and some who know supportive trans adults who are also questioning recent theories of 'transgenderism.'

"When Children Say They're Trans:
Hormones? Surgery? The choices are fraught—and there are no easy answers."

by Jesse Singal, *The Atlantic*, July/August 2018

Quotes from the article:

How can parents get children the support they might need while keeping in mind that adolescence is, by definition, a time of identity exploration?

"I'm a real-live 22-year-old woman with a scarred chest and a broken voice and a 5 o'clock shadow because I couldn't face the idea of growing up to be a woman," said Cari Stella, a detransitioner.

https://www.theatlantic.com/magazine/archive/2018/07/when-a-child-says-shes-trans/561749/

Ask Me First MN Parent Resource Guide

Includes resources, tips, and talking points that will help parents be better equipped to understand and counter harmful policies being enacted in schools.

http://www.mfc.org/parent-resource-guide/

Sources of more detransition stories

TranZformed:
Finding Peace with Your God-Given Gender

by Pure Passion Media (2016)

Fifteen ex-transgender individuals join with numerous experts to dispel the confusion and bear witness to what

Jesus Christ can do for those who struggle with gender dysphoria.

Video available at tranZformed.org

Real-Life Victims of the Transgender 'Cult'

by Tyler O'Neil, PJ Media (2016)

More and more parents are stepping out, admitting that their children "identify as transgender" and wanting to do something about it. Schools encourage gender confusion, and doctors reportedly won't even run preliminary tests if a child asks for life-altering "treatment." But before you sign your kids up, listen to the real-life stories of people who deeply regret their "transition."

pjmedia.com/parenting/2016/08/21/real-life-victims-of-the-transgender-cult/

"I Want My Sex Back"

Powerful documentary profiles transgender regret
by RT Documentary (2018)

Detransitioned transgender people who regret changing sex speak out. Billy, Rene and Walt were born male, but they all felt uncomfortable with their sex. So, they underwent sex reassignment surgery, believing it would end their distressing condition, which is known as gender dysphoria—feeling uncomfortable with one's birth sex.

https://youtu.be/0R7DXnqkfJw

Resources from Walt Heyer

Paper Genders:
Pulling the Mask Off the Transgender Phenomenon

by Walt Heyer (2011)

Paper Genders debunks the glowing promises of gender change surgery and exposes the heart-breaking story of suicide and wrecked lives that the advocates would prefer to keep hidden. Profoundly clear, well-documented and fair.

Gender, Lies and Suicide

by Walt Heyer (2013)

Patients with gender dysphoria undergo hormone injections and irreversible surgeries in a desperate effort to feel better, yet they attempt and commit suicide at an alarming rate, even after treatment. Walt Heyer digs into the issues behind transgender suicide and shares some heart-wrenching letters from those who regret the decision to change genders.

A Transgender's Faith

by Walt Heyer (2015)

Man to woman and back again—a personal story The powerful testimony of one man's faith and restoration to his birth gender.

Websites by Walt Heyer

SexChangeRegret.com

WaltHeyer.com

ATransgendersFaith.com

Articles by Walt Heyer

Walt Heyer has written over 50 articles on transgender topics for the following publications:

ThePublicDiscourse.com/author/walt-heyer/

TheFederalist.com/author/walt-heyer/

DailySignal.com/author/walt-heyer/